The Federal Wage & Hour Laws

SECOND EDITION

The Federal Wage & Hour Laws

SECOND EDITION

| R. BRIAN DIXON |

THE SOCIETY FOR HUMAN RESOURCE MANAGEMENT
ALEXANDRIA, VIRGINIA
USA
WWW.SHRM.ORG

#5157946S

This publication is designed to provide accurate and authoritative information regarding the subject matter covered. It is sold with the understanding that neither the publisher nor the author is engaged in rendering legal or other professional service. If legal advice or other expert assistance is required, the services of a competent, licensed professional should be sought. The federal and state laws discussed in this book are subject to frequent revision and interpretation by amendments or judicial revisions that may significantly affect employer or employee rights and obligations. Readers are encouraged to seek legal counsel regarding specific policies and practices in their organizations. We are confident that the information contained herein is accurate and up-to-date through February 2002.

This book is published by the Society for Human Resource Management (SHRM). The interpretations, conclusions, and recommendations in this book are those of the author and do not necessarily represent those of SHRM or the SHRM Foundation.

The Society for Human Resource Management is the world's largest association devoted to human resource management. Representing more than 165,000 individual members, the Society's mission is both to serve human resource management professionals and to advance the profession. Visit SHRM Online at www.shrm.org.

The SHRM Foundation is the catalyst for leading-edge research and information to advance the human resource profession. As the nonprofit affiliate of the Society for Human Resource Management, the SHRM Foundation helps raise the standards of performance in the profession through its support of research, publications, and educational initiatives. Visit the SHRM Foundation Online at www.shrm.org/foundation.

Cover and interior design by Fan Works Design

ISBN 1-58644-019-5

Printed in the United States of America.
10 9 8 7 6 5 4 3 2 1

02-0130

TABLE OF CONTENTS

Chapter 12

WHAT IS THE PREVAILING WAGE OBLIGATION? 99

INTRODUCTION

The Fair Labor Standards Act was passed in 1938 to establish a minimum wage and overtime pay obligation. The original minimum wage was 25 cents per hour, and overtime was due after 44 hours of work in a week. Today the Fair Labor Standards Act (FLSA) provides a minimum wage of $5.15 per hour, and overtime is due after 40 hours of work in a week. In addition, many states have enacted minimum wage and overtime requirements, which are, in some instances, more restrictive than those imposed by federal law. These laws have been supplemented by other wage-and-hour laws that apply to employees engaged on government contracts and in other limited circumstances.

The Fair Labor Standards Act

The resolution of any issue concerning an employer's obligations under the FLSA entails a consideration of the following questions:

- Is the employer subject to the FLSA?
- Is there an employment relationship?
- Is the activity at issue considered work?
- What is the minimum wage obligation?
- What is the overtime obligation?
- Is the employee exempt from the receipt of the minimum wage or overtime?
- When is child labor permitted?
- What is the equal pay obligation?
- What records must be kept?
- What wage payment obligations exist?
- How are the wage and hour laws enforced?
- What is the prevailing wage obligation?

Each of these questions is the subject of one of the following chapters.

Additional Sources of Federal Regulation

The federal government has set higher wage payment standards with respect to work that is performed under government contracts. Special minimum prevailing wage obligations are imposed under the Davis-Bacon Act for employers that engage in federally financed construction, the Walsh-Healey Act for employers that supply goods or materials to the federal government, and the Service Contract Labor Standards Act for employers that contract to provide services to the federal government. The federal Contract Work Hours and Safety Standards Act imposes a 40-hour-per-week overtime standard for laborers and mechanics engaged on federal projects. These prevailing wage obligations are the subject of the last chapter in the book.

This book does not address federal statutes that are peripheral to the payment of wages, such as the Migrant and Seasonal Agricultural Worker Protection Act, 29 U.S.C. §§ 1801, *et seq.*, 29 C.F.R. pt. 500; the Family and Medical Leave Act, 29 U.S.C. §§ 2601, *et seq.*, 29 C.F.R.

pt. 825; and the Consumer Credit Protection Act, 15 U.S.C. §§ 1673, *et seq.*, 29 C.F.R. pt. 870.

The Relationship Between State and Federal Wage and Hour Laws

With the growth of state regulation, an employer must be mindful of the obligations that are imposed by each of the states in which the employer does business. Most states model their minimum wage and overtime requirements on the obligations imposed by federal law. However, variations do exist, and the exact scope of those variations exceeds the objective of this book. The book does alert employers to those circumstances in which a difference is most likely to exist. The questions that are set out in the first section regarding the FLSA may serve as a model by which an employer can resolve its obligations under the laws of the various states.

As a general rule, federal wage and hour laws do *not* preempt state laws. 29 U.S.C. § 218(a). Thus, an employer must comply with the more stringent of the minimum wage and overtime standards that are imposed by the FLSA or those that are imposed by state law. An employee who is exempt from either federal or state law, but not both, must be paid in accordance with whichever law applies.

Limited exceptions exist to the rule that the states are free, regardless of federal law, to regulate employees' compensation. For example, the federal government's comprehensive regulation of railroads has been found to preempt state regulation of railroad employees' wages, and federal admiralty law has been found to preempt state regulation of the wages of seamen who engage in foreign, intercoastal, and coastwise voyages.

Use of This Book

The application of the FLSA to every type of employment relationship has resulted in a large and complex body of regulations and court decisions. This book includes references to the provisions of the Act and to the regulations of the Department of Labor. Because this book necessarily summarizes an employer's obligations, it is important for an employer to consult the regulations and case law before relying on any exemption from the Act's obligations. Employers must always ascertain their obligations under state law as well as federal law.

The following abbreviations are used in this book. *FLSA* or *Act* refers to the Fair Labor Standards Act, 29 U.S.C. §§ 201, *et seq*. The United States Department of Labor is sometimes referred to as the *DOL*. The *United States Code* is referred to as *U.S.C.*, and the *Code of Federal Regulations* is referred to as *C.F.R.* A section in the codes is referred to as §, and a part of the codes is referred to as *pt*. The provisions of the *United States Code* and the *Code of Federal Regulations* that are enforced by the Department of Labor can be found at <www.dol.gov>.

Chapter 1

Is the Employer Subject to the Fair Labor Standards Act?

The FLSA applies to virtually all public employers and most private employers. Even if the FLSA does not apply to all employees of an employer, the Act may still apply to individual employees who are involved in interstate commerce.

When Is a Public Employer Subject to the Constraints of the FLSA?

The term *employer* under the FLSA includes all *public agencies*. Public agencies include the federal government, state governments, subdivisions and agencies of the federal and state governments, the United States Postal Service, and the Government Printing Office. 29 U.S.C. §§ 203(s)(1), (x). Although the FLSA nominally applies to state employees, the states are immune from FLSA claims in federal court and are immune from FLSA claims in their own courts, unless a state has waived its sovereign immunity. This immunity from suit does not extend to lesser public entities such as counties and cities. The application of the FLSA to public employers is further limited by exclusions from the definition of *employee*. As a result of this definition of the Act's scope, all employees of the federal government and of local government entities will be covered by the FLSA unless they fall within one of the narrow exclusions from the definition of *employee*. These exclusions are discussed in chapter 2.

When Is a Private Employer Subject to the Constraints of the FLSA?

Private employers are subject to the FLSA if they are engaged in interstate commerce *and either* exceed specified dollar volumes of business *or* are engaged in certain industries. The FLSA's definition of interstate commerce is very broad. For example, an employer is considered to be engaged in interstate commerce if its employees *handle* or in any way *work on* goods that *have moved* in interstate commerce. 29 U.S.C. § 203(j), (s). The test of participation in interstate commerce is so broad that virtually every employer that meets the dollar volume of business standard is covered by the Act.

All of the employees of an enterprise that is engaged in interstate commerce will be subject to regulation by the FLSA. An *enterprise* includes all of the related activities that are conducted by separate business entities if the businesses are joined together through either unified operation or common control to serve a common business purpose. 29 U.S.C. § 203(r)(1). The fact that several entities are separately owned or incorporated will not preclude their being found to be a single enterprise if the other elements of the definition are met. An independently owned retail or service establishment, however, will not be considered to be part of an enterprise simply because the establishment has agreed to purchase or sell a particular manufacturer's goods. 29 U.S.C. § 203(r)(1). Similarly, an independently owned retail or service establishment will not be considered to be part of an enterprise simply because the establishment has leased premises from a person who leases other premises to other retail and service establishments.

Effective April 1, 1990, enterprises are subject to the Act if their annual dollar volume of business exceeds $500,000 per year, exclusive of excise taxes. 29 U.S.C. § 203(s)(1). Hospitals and institutions that are primarily engaged in the care of the sick, the aged, the mentally ill, or the developmentally disabled who reside on the premises of the institution are covered by the Act regardless of their annual dollar volume of business and their status as profit or nonprofit entities. Schools for developmentally disabled or gifted children, preschools, elementary and secondary schools, and institutions of higher learning are also covered by the Act regardless of their annual dollar volume of business and profit or nonprofit status. An enterprise that was subject to the Act before April 1, 1990, must continue to pay the minimum wage that was then in effect and to comply with the other obligations that are imposed by the Act, even if the enterprise is no longer covered by the Act. Before April 1, 1990, the Act covered all construction, laundry, and dry cleaning businesses regardless of their volume of business. Before April 1, 1990, the FLSA also applied to retail and service businesses that had an annual sales volume of $362,500 and to other businesses that had an annual sales volume of $250,000 or more, exclusive of excise taxes. The minimum wage in 1990 was $3.35 per hour.

Employers who are not otherwise covered by the Act must pay the minimum wage to all of their employees if they have contracted to provide services to the United States government. 29 U.S.C. § 206(e). Only white-collar employees and employees who spend entire workweeks outside the United States are excluded from this minimum wage obligation.

Any physically separate business establishment that employs only the parents, spouse, children, or other immediate family members of the owner will not be considered to be an enterprise engaged in interstate commerce. 29 U.S.C. § 203(s)(2). The sales of such an establishment cannot be combined with the sales of any other entity in order to meet the dollar volume of business test. However, individual employees of such a small business may still be covered by the Act if the individual employees are directly engaged in interstate commerce or in the production of goods for interstate commerce.

When Must an Employer Apply the FLSA to Individual Employees?

The FLSA may cover individual employees even if their employer does *not* conduct a sufficient volume of business so as to have all of its employees covered by the FLSA. 29 U.S.C. §§ 206(a), 207(a). The Act applies to all employees who are engaged in the instrumentalities of interstate commerce such as transportation and telecommunications. The Act also applies to employees who are directly engaged in the production of goods for interstate commerce, such as goods that are shipped directly out of state. The production of goods for interstate commerce includes manufacturing, mining, handling, or otherwise working on goods that leave the state. Those employees who produce such goods and those who are employed in the occupations that are directly essential to the production of such goods are covered by the Act. 29 U.S.C. § 203(j).

The Act specifically covers the employment of domestic employees. 29 U.S.C. § 206(f). Domestic employees such as cooks, maids, and chauffeurs will be covered if they earn more than the annual social security threshold, which was $1,000 in 1995 and is adjusted annually. Domestic employees are also covered if they work, for all of their employers in the aggregate, more than 8 hours per week. Domestic employees must be paid overtime unless they reside on their employer's premises. 29 U.S.C. §§ 207(l), 213(b)(21).

When Is a Manager Considered to Be an Employer?

The FLSA's definition of an *employer* is structured so as to make agents of employers who have decision-making responsibility for wage payment practices *personally* liable for the minimum wage and overtime obligations imposed by the Act. 29 U.S.C. § 203(d). A manager need not have an ownership interest in a business in order to be found to be an employer. State law rarely imposes such personal liability.

When Are Two Nominally Separate Entities a Joint Employer?

A common-law joint-employer relationship is recognized under the FLSA. The standards used to establish such a relationship have not been precisely defined, but they include a consideration of matters such as whether any agreement exists to share the employee's services, whether services are provided to both employers at the same time, whether both entities are commonly controlled, and the like. 29 C.F.R. pt. 791. If an individual works for two nominally separate entities that are actually joint employers, the individual's hours of work must be summed to determine when overtime is due and whether the minimum wage obligation has been met. Both entities will be jointly liable for any wages that are due.

When Is a Successor Employer Liable for a Predecessor's Conduct?

A common-law successor relationship has recently been recognized under the FLSA. Whether one employer is a successor to another is generally determined by considering whether the alleged successor uses the same employees and supervisors, provides the same services or products, operates from the same location and with the same equipment, and otherwise acts as a continuation of the predecessor's business. To be liable as a successor employer, the successor must have had notice of the predecessor's failure to comply with the FLSA. Where there is such a continuity of business and notice of the previous failure to pay wages, the successor may be held liable for the predecessor's failure to pay all wages due. However, such liability may be avoided if it is shown that, absent the successor's purchase of a failing predecessor, the employment relationships at issue would not have continued because the predecessor would have gone out of business.

Chapter 2

Is There an Employment Relationship?

For the FLSA to apply, an employer-employee relationship must exist. Under the Act, *to employ* means *to suffer or permit to work*. 29 U.S.C. § 203(g). This definition is very broad, and it is often easy for an employment relationship to be created. For example, individuals who provide services to an employer will be found to be employees where the benefits of such services accrue to the employer and the employer could have discovered who was rendering such services through the exercise of reasonable diligence.

Individuals Who Are Not Employees

The principal statutory exclusions from the FLSA's definition of *employee* concern certain government employees. 29 U.S.C. § 203(e). Most individuals who work for the federal government are considered to be employees.

29 U.S.C. § 203(e)(2)(A); 2 U.S.C. § 1313. Most federal employees are also subject to the provisions of the Federal Employee Pay Act, 5 U.S.C. §§ 5541, *et seq.* The compensation of federal employees is generally regulated by the Office of Personnel Management.

Most state and local government employees are also subject to the FLSA. The few state and local government employees excluded from the FLSA are those who are not subject to civil service laws and who either are elected to office or are appointed by elected officials to personal staff, immediate advisor, or policy-making positions. 29 U.S.C. § 203(e)(2)(C). Employees who work in the legislative branches of state and local governments are also excluded if they are not subject to civil service laws and are not employed by the legislative library. The ability of state employees to obtain remedies for violation of the Act, however, may be restricted by the limited jurisdiction of the federal and state courts.

The definition of *employee* specifically excludes certain volunteer activities of public employees and implicitly excludes certain individuals who volunteer to provide services to private employers. Employees of interstate, state, and local public agencies who volunteer to perform services without any compensation, or in exchange for the receipt of an expense reimbursement, reasonable benefits, or a nominal fee, are considered to be volunteers and not employees while performing such services. 29 U.S.C. § 203(e)(4)(A). The exclusion of such services from employment applies only to the extent that the services are of a type different from those the individual is employed to perform for the agency. An employee of an interstate, state, or local public agency may also volunteer to perform services for a public agency different from that which employs the individual. 29 U.S.C. § 203(e)(4)(B). Such volunteer activities may include the performance of services under a mutual aid agreement between the two agencies.

An individual who volunteers services solely for humanitarian purposes to private, nonprofit food banks is not an employee. 29 U.S.C. § 203(e)(5). The individual's receipt of groceries from the food bank does not affect the exclusion from employment.

Volunteers who provide services to private employers are also not considered to be employees. *Volunteers* are generally limited to individuals who provide services without any expectation of payment for public service or humanitarian purposes, such as providing support to patients in a hospital. The regular employees of a private employer cannot volunteer to perform work for their employer without compensation unless the work is of a humanitarian nature and unrelated to the employee's regular job.

The only common, nonstatutory exclusion from employee status under the FLSA concerns trainees or interns. *Trainees* are individuals who, under the following specific, limited criteria, are engaged in work-study programs:

- The training is for the benefit of the trainees or the interns.
- The trainees do not displace regular employees but work under close observation.
- The employer that provides the training derives no immediate advantage from the activities of the trainees or interns, and, on occasion, its operations actually may be impeded.
- The trainees or the students are not necessarily entitled to a job at the completion of the training period.
- The employer and the trainees or interns understand that the trainees or interns are not entitled to wages for the time spent in training.

Individuals are most likely to be considered to be trainees or interns if they are also engaged in work-study programs of a professional nature.

The few other nonstatutory exclusions from the definition of an employee illustrate how broad the definition of employment is. Inmates who are required to work in prison industries have been found consistently not to be employees, although there is still some latitude for finding an employment relationship with prisoners. The law enforcement and government employees of American Indian tribes have also been found to be excluded from the Act.

Independent Contractors

Wage and hour laws apply only where an employer-employee relationship exists; an independent contractor is not considered to be an employee. All individuals who are *economically dependent* on a company are employees of the company. This broad definition of *employee* contained in the FLSA has left a correspondingly narrow area within which an individual will be regarded as an independent contractor. An individual will *not* be found to be an independent contractor merely because the individual has agreed to be an independent contractor; independent contractors are substantively different from employees. In determining whether an individual is an employee or an independent contractor, the courts consider the following factors:

- The degree of control exercised by the alleged employer,
- The extent of the relative investments of the worker and alleged employer,
- The degree to which the worker's opportunity for profit and loss is determined by the alleged employer,
- The skill and initiative required in performing the job, and
- The permanency of the relationship.

These factors are merely aids in determining the underlying question of economic dependency, and no single factor is determinative. Other factors may also be considered. In an appraisal of whether an individual is an employee or a contractor, the focus will be on what the individual actually did in the relationship, not what the individual could have done. A growing tendency exists to consider individuals who work for brief periods of time to be casual employees rather than independent contractors.

The broad definition of employment under the FLSA is exemplified by the conclusion that individuals who leased dry cleaning outlets and purchased the stock of the preceding lessee were employees. The individuals were found to be employees because the lessor of the outlet required all of the dry cleaning to be processed in its plant, set the prices that could be charged, regulated the hours of operation, and the like.

Most state labor statutes contain the narrower *common-law* definition of an independent contractor. Under the common-law test, an independent contractor is generally one who accomplishes a specified task for a specified price and retains the right to control the manner in which the work is accomplished. However, the criteria that are used to determine whether a meaningful right to control exists have expanded over time to include many of the above criteria. Thus, a state court may well define an independent contractor in terms commensurate with those of the FLSA.

Homeworkers

Individuals who regularly perform work from home for a company are likely to be found to be employees. The DOL has vigorously and successfully litigated any contention that such individuals can be considered to be independent contractors. The DOL's regulations prohibit the manufacture of women's garments, jewelry, and related items by employees in their homes without certificates for each employee from the DOL. 29 C.F.R. pt. 530. The DOL otherwise believes that allowing employees to work from home promotes an appropriate balance between work and family. The DOL may require additional records of homeworkers' hours of work. States may regulate the employment of individuals at home, particularly in the making of goods, more stringently than does the federal government.

Chapter 3

IS THE ACTIVITY AT ISSUE CONSIDERED WORK?

To comply with its minimum wage and overtime obligations, an employer must accurately define which of its employees' activities are considered hours of work.

Work Time

All time spent in an employee's principal duties and all essential ancillary activities must be counted as *work time*. An employee's principal duties include an employee's productive tasks. Ancillary activities, such as maintaining equipment, loading or fueling a vehicle, receiving instructions, distributing work, and preparing work materials, are also generally compensable work activities. All time spent in such duties, whether spent on or off the employer's premises or before or after regular work hours, is counted as work time.

An employee's work time is generally compensable if expended for the employer's benefit, if controlled by the employer, or if allowed by the employer. An employer's refusal to authorize overtime work, however, will *not* prevent an employee from recovering pay for such work if the work was known or should have been known by the employer. If an employer wishes to avoid payment for work that is not authorized, then the employer must act affirmatively to put a stop to the work.

Activities that occur before or after an employee's principal duties, and that are not subject to compensation by the terms of an express contract or custom or practice, need not be counted as work time. 29 U.S.C. § 254(a), (b). However, the general rule remains that activities that are part of, or substantially related to, the employee's principal duties are compensable. For example, a butcher who is sharpening his or her tools is considered to be working even if the butcher customarily has not been paid for tool sharpening.

These basic principles regarding the definition of work time have been applied to the various aspects of the employment relationship such as clothes changing, travel, and the like. Those aspects of the employment relationship that are considered to be work are described below.

Clothes Changing and Washing

Clothes changing and washing time is generally not compensable unless required by the nature of the job, such as handling toxic chemicals; required by the employer or by law to occur at the work site. Clothes changing and washing time is work time if the employer pays for the time. Clothes changing and washing time that occurs at the beginning or end of the workday may be eliminated from hours worked by the terms of or the practice under a collective bargaining agreement. 29 U.S.C. § 203(o). Time spent changing clothes at home is not work time, even if the employer requires an employee to wear specified clothing to work.

Travel Time

Travel time to and from work is generally not compensable. 29 C.F.R. § 785.35. Employees who drive vehicles that contain significant amounts of tools or equipment from their homes to work sites are working while traveling. However, travel from home to work in a company vehicle and any activities incidental to such travel will not be work time if so agreed with the employee or the employee's representative and if the travel is within the normal commuting area for the employer's business or establishment. For such travel to be nonwork time, the company vehicle must be provided at no cost to the employee. Travel from home to a customer's site in response to an emergency call after the regular workday is work time. 29 C.F.R. § 785.36.

Employees who travel in the course of a workday, such as from one work location to another, are entitled to compensation for their travel time. 29 C.F.R. § 785.38. For example, an employee who reports to a construction company's shop to obtain instructions or to load a truck is considered to have performed some work, and the employee's subsequent travel to a job site will be considered work time. If an employee regularly works at different sites, single-day travel to those sites may not be work time.

Travel out of town may also be considered work. When an employee who normally works at one location is sent out of town on a single-day trip, the time spent traveling is work time. 29 C.F.R. § 785.37. However, the employer may consider the time spent traveling to and from the airport or other transportation terminal in the morning and evening to be the equivalent of the home-to-work commute and not compensable work time. The difference between compensable single-day, out-of-town travel and noncompensable home-to-work travel of employees who travel long distances to work is not well defined.

An employee who travels away from home overnight is not working when he or she is a passenger on an airplane, train, boat, bus, or automobile outside the employee's regular work hours. 29 C.F.R. § 785.39. Any time that the employee spends traveling as a passenger on a weekday or on a weekend will be counted as work time if the travel cuts across the hours the employee would normally work during the week. Any time an employee spends working while a passenger must be counted and paid as work time.

Meal Periods

Meal periods are not work time if they are 30 minutes or longer, if the employee is relieved of all duties, and if the employee is free to leave his or her workstation. A meal period is not compensable, even if an employee is unable to leave the premises. Special rules apply to fire protection and law enforcement personnel who are paid overtime under the relaxed standards discussed in chapter 6. 29 C.F.R. § 553.223.

Sleep Time

Sleep time can be excluded from work time only if an employee is on duty for 24 hours, the employee can usually enjoy an uninterrupted night's sleep, the employee has reasonable sleeping facilities, not more than 8 hours of sleep are excluded from any 24-hour period, and the employee has agreed to exclude sleep time from compensable hours of work. 29 C.F.R. § 785.22. Any interruption of sleep to return to work must be counted as work time, and the entire sleep period must be counted as work time if the employee receives less than 5 hours of sleep. The requirement that an employee be on duty for 24 hours for sleep time to be excluded does not apply to employees who reside on their employer's premises. 29 C.F.R. § 785.23. Again, special rules apply to fire protection and law enforcement personnel who are paid overtime under the relaxed standard that can be applied to such employees. 29 C.F.R. § 553.222.

On-Call and Standby Time

On-call time and standby time are not compensable if the employee can use the time spent on call primarily for his or her own benefit. 29 C.F.R. § 785.17. Considerations in determining whether such time is work time include the following:

* Whether employees are free to go where they wish while on standby, either by leaving a telephone number with their employer or by using a paging device;

- Whether employees are called to work so frequently that they lose the ability to engage in activities of their own choice;
- Whether employees are obligated to respond to every call or only need to respond to a reasonable number of calls;
- Whether employees have, after receipt of a mandatory call to return to work, enough time to disengage from their personal activities so that the employees feel free to undertake a reasonable range of activities while on call;
- Whether the disciplinary consequences of an employee's failure to respond to any call to return to work are so severe that the employee must constantly be prepared to return to work;
- Whether employees are on standby for so many consecutive hours that they are never able to engage in activities that can be pursued only while off standby;
- Whether the employees must respond to miscellaneous work-related telephone calls while on standby;
- Whether employees can readily trade on-call responsibilities;
- Whether the need to use a particular vehicle to respond to calls limits the employee's activities;
- The scope of personal activities actually undertaken while on call;
- Any agreement as to whether or not the on-call time is work time; and
- Any other circumstances that create a burden on the employee's use of his or her own time.

If an employee is required to wait at the employer's premises or at a particular location other than the employee's home, all of the waiting time must be counted as hours of work. Employees may be found to be working while on call even when not confined to their homes. For example, employees were found to be working 24 hours a day while on call because they had to be within radio range, listen to the radio, and respond to calls within 30 minutes. In another case, however, an employee was *not* found to be working while on 24-hour-a-day, 7-day-per-week pager call even though the employee had to return to the hospital within 20 minutes of being called. Given the absence of consensus, employers must exercise particular care in this area.

Break Periods

Whether a break period during which an employee is relieved of all duty in a workday can be considered to be noncompensable turns on whether the employee can use the period of time for his or her own benefit. Brief breaks of up to 20 minutes are considered to be work time. 29 C.F.R. § 785.16. An employee who requests a break of more than 20 minutes to conduct personal business will generally not be working during the break. A break of 20 minutes or more that is initiated by an employer may be considered compensable waiting time.

Waiting Time

Waiting time may be work time depending on the circumstances. Waiting to start work after arriving early is not work time unless the employer required the employee to arrive early. If an employer delays the start of regular work, the waiting time is likely to be work time. Waiting to punch out after finishing work for the day is not work time unless the employer causes an unusual delay in the process of leaving the premises. Waiting between periods of work during the workday, other than *bona fide* meal periods, will be work time unless the employee is relieved of all duty, is free to leave the premises, and is told of a specific time to return and the time is long enough for the employee to use it primarily for his or her own benefit. 29 C.F.R. § 785.18. Depending on the circumstances, waiting time of up to 2 hours has been found to be work time.

Training

An employee's attendance at employment-related training programs will be considered to be work time unless attendance is outside of regular work hours, attendance is in fact voluntary, no productive work is performed during the training, and the training is not directed at making the employee more proficient in the individual's present job. 29 C.F.R.

§ 785.27. If the training is of a type that is generalized in nature and is commensurate with training that would be acquired through an independent educational facility, then the last requirement is excused. Attendance outside of regular work hours at specialized or follow-up training that is necessary for an employee to maintain certification in his or her occupation and that the employee is required by law to complete is not generally considered work time. 29 C.F.R. § 553.226. Time spent in supplemental instruction as a part of an approved apprenticeship training program also may not be work time. Time voluntarily spent in training outside of regular work hours for a future promotional position is not considered to be work time even if the training is specific to the future job.

Meetings

Whether time spent in meetings between management and employees is work time must be resolved on a case-by-case basis. Generally, the time spent in required meetings with management and the time spent while employees are required to be on premises during regular work hours to adjust grievances are work time. 29 C.F.R. § 785.42. The time spent just discussing grievances may not be work time if it occurs outside the regular workday. If the employees work under a union contract, the terms of the contract or the custom and practice under the contract will determine the compensability of such time. Attending internal union meetings is generally not compensable work time.

Attending industry meetings and conferences is work time if the employer requires attendance or sponsors the event. An employer's arrangement of travel to and attendance at such meetings will contribute to a finding that the time is compensable work. Attendance is not work time if it is voluntarily undertaken by an employee outside of regular work hours and the time is not otherwise compensable training time.

Vacation, Holiday, and Sick Leave

Time for which an employer pays but during which an employee performs no work is not counted as hours of work. As a result, payment for the time that is spent on vacation, holiday, and sick leave need not be counted toward the threshold after which overtime must be paid. An employer may count such paid time off as work time. If the employer does so, the amount paid will be included in the regular rate of pay.

Medical Examinations

Preemployment medical examinations do not count as hours worked. Time spent at a medical appointment is hours worked if medical attention is received during regular work hours and the appointment is completed on the employer's premises or the employer directs where the appointment is to be conducted. 29 C.F.R. § 785.43. If the employee elects treatment off the employer's premises or the employee elects to conduct an appointment with a company medical representative outside of regular work hours, the time spent in the appointment is not compensable work time. After an individual is hired, time spent in legally required medical appointments such as those required by the Department of Transportation is generally considered by the DOL to be work time.

Hours of Work for Public Employees

The hours of work for public employees are defined under the FLSA in essentially the same terms as those used for private employees. As noted above, some special rules apply for fire protection and law enforcement personnel, which are discussed in chapter 6. The number of hours of work after which a public employee is due overtime may also be affected by the partial overtime exemptions for special detail work, occasional and sporadic employment, and substituting for coworkers, which are discussed in chapter 6. The number of hours worked by employees of interstate, state, and local public agencies may be affected by the expanded definition of *volunteers*, which is discussed in chapter 2.

Chapter 4

What Is the Minimum Wage Obligation?

The minimum wage is intended to provide a minimally acceptable level of compensation for employees. The decision to implement a minimum wage reflects a congressional determination that it is better to forgo the provision of certain marginal employment opportunities in order to strengthen other employment relationships.

How Is Compliance With the Minimum Wage Calculated?

Compliance with the minimum wage and the overtime provisions of the FLSA is computed on a workweek that consists of seven consecutive 24-hour periods. The minimum wage obligation under the Act will be met if the compensation for a workweek, when divided by the hours worked that week, is equal to or greater than the minimum wage. Wages paid in excess of the minimum for one workweek are generally not creditable toward underpayments in other weeks. The federal minimum wage became $5.15 per hour on September 1, 1997. 29 U.S.C. § 206(a).

Special minimum piece rates may apply to homeworkers in Puerto Rico and the Virgin Islands. 29 U.S.C. § 206(a).

The minimum wage of employees in American Samoa is subject to regulation by wage orders that are issued by the DOL. 29 U.S.C. § 206(a)(3). The DOL must consult with industry committees regarding wage rates in American Samoa before issuing wage orders, and the validity of the orders is subject to a special court review process. 29 U.S.C. §§ 205, 208, 210.

Employees who are less than 20 years of age may be paid $4.25 during the first 90 calendar days of employment if no other employees are displaced. 29 U.S.C. § 206(g).

Various exemptions exist for employing learners, apprentices, messengers, students, and disabled workers at less than the minimum wage rate. 29 U.S.C. § 214(a)–(d). There are also a number of other exemptions from both the minimum wage and overtime. These exemptions are discussed in chapter 6.

What Sources of Income Can Be Credited Toward the Minimum Wage?

Employers may count as wages paid to their employees the *fair value* or the *reasonable cost* to the employer of meals, lodging, transportation, and other services as long as the facilities or services are for the employee's benefit and are customarily provided to employees in the industry. 29 C.F.R. pt. 531. The requirement that an employee voluntarily accept payments in kind has been successfully disputed with respect to the FLSA. However, state laws may limit the amounts that can be credited against the minimum wage and the circumstances in which a credit can be taken. For example, California requires a voluntary written agreement before any credit can be taken for meals or lodging.

Employers cannot count toward the minimum wage the cost of tools provided for the employee's use in the employer's business; the cost of purchasing, renting, or laundering required uniforms; or the cost of transportation that is provided for the employer's benefit. 29 C.F.R. pt. 531. The distinction between a required uniform and a dress code is a fine one. If an employer's dress code is too restrictive, the employer will be required to pay the amount by which the purchase of the clothing reduces the employee's wage below the minimum.

Employers also cannot credit toward the minimum wage any compensation that is excluded from the regular rate of pay. 29 U.S.C. § 207(h)(1). The regular rate of pay is discussed in chapter 5.

If an employee regularly earns at least $30.00 per month in tips, the employer may credit the amount of the tips received toward the minimum wage, but the amount credited cannot exceed the difference between the minimum wage then in effect and $4.25 per hour. 29 U.S.C. § 203(m), (t). The employer must give notice that tips will be counted toward the minimum wage before the employer takes any credit for the tips. Some states, such as Oregon, prohibit such tip credits.

State Regulation of the Minimum Wage

The states are free to set a minimum wage higher than that required by the FLSA. In Washington the minimum wage is, as of January 1, 2002, $6.90 per hour, and in Oregon the minimum wage is now $6.50 per hour.

Chapter 5

WHAT IS THE OVERTIME OBLIGATION?

The FLSA does not limit the hours that an employee can work, but the Act does require that an employee be compensated for all of the hours worked in the workweek. The obligation to pay overtime indirectly limits an employee's hours of work and provides an incentive to create additional employment opportunities.

How Is the Overtime Obligation Different From the Minimum Wage Obligation?

The resolution of an overtime problem entails concepts that are fundamentally different from those required to resolve a minimum wage problem. As noted previously, the sole issue entailed in resolving a minimum wage problem under the FLSA is a mechanistic determination: whether the compensation received for the week, when divided by the hours worked, exceeds the minimum wage. The satisfaction of an employer's overtime obligation turns not only on the amount paid, but also on the labels and conditions attached to the payments that are made. The ultimate objective of overtime legislation is to force an increase in the rate of an employee's compensation to occur after a specified number of hours of work. Inasmuch as the change in compensation can be accomplished (or subverted) by juggling the employee's underlying rate of compensation, the search for the employee's rate of compensation *in fact*, the employee's *regular rate*, is of primary importance.

What Is the Basic Overtime Obligation?

The FLSA generally requires that an employee be paid an additional one half of the individual's regular rate for all hours of work in excess of 40 in a week. 29 U.S.C. § 207(a). An employer can contract to pay overtime for fewer hours of work but is not required to do so. An employee or an employee's union representative *cannot waive* overtime pay due under the FLSA.

The hours that are counted when determining whether overtime is due are determined by a workweek of seven consecutive 24-hour periods. The hours worked cannot be averaged across more than one workweek. An employer is obligated to record the workweek that it uses. An employer need not use the same workweek for all employees. A workweek, once chosen, is expected to remain in effect relatively indefinitely. If an employer changes the workweek, a special one-time calculation of overtime should be made. 29 C.F.R. §§ 778.301, 778.302.

There are both complete exemptions from the payment of overtime, such as those for executive, administrative, professional, and outside sales employees, and partial exemptions from the payment of overtime, such as those for employees of health facilities who are paid overtime after 8 hours of work in a day and 80 hours in a 14-day work period. These complete and partial exemptions are discussed in chapter 6.

What Special Rules Exist for Public Employees?

State and local government employers have some additional latitude when calculating overtime. The broad definition of a volunteer, which is described in chapter 2, and the exclusion of work on special details, occasional and sporadic work, and substituting for coworkers, which are described in chapter 6, limit the circumstances in which overtime must be paid to public employees. Of greater importance are the special overtime rules for fire protection and law enforcement personnel, which are also discussed in chapter 6.

How Do Employers Meet the Overtime Obligation?

The *only* way to satisfy the federal overtime obligation is to pay the overtime premium. Providing fringe benefits such as health insurance or retirement plans will not satisfy the overtime obligation. Paying a salary or a higher-than-normal hourly wage also will not satisfy the overtime obligation. Compensation by piece rate or commission does not discharge the obligation to pay overtime unless the piece rates or commissions are increased by one half after 40 hours of work in a week or the piece rates or commissions are included in the calculation of overtime. Paying the higher of *either* commissions or piece rates without overtime *or* a low hourly rate with overtime generally will not discharge the obligation to pay overtime. Although, as discussed below, public employers can use compensatory time off in lieu of overtime, it is difficult for private employers to do so.

Compensatory Time Off for Public Employees

The FLSA provides an element of flexibility for state and local government employers and a choice for their employees regarding compensation for overtime work. A public employer may provide compensatory time off ("comp time") in lieu of monetary overtime compensation, at a rate of not less than one and one half hours of compensatory time off for each hour of overtime worked. 29 U.S.C. § 207(o); 29 C.F.R. § 553.20.

The use of comp time is allowed as long as it is provided for under a collective bargaining agreement, employment agreement, or memorandum of understanding. The agreement or understanding to use compensatory time off must be arrived at before the performance of work. 29 C.F.R. § 553.23(a). The agreement can be made in one of three ways: through negotiation with individual employees, through negotiation with employees' representatives, or through negotiation with a recognized collective bargaining agent. 29 C.F.R. § 553.23. If it was the employer's practice before April 15, 1985, to pay existing employees compensatory time, that practice will suffice as an understanding that permits the use of compensatory time.

The use of compensatory time off in lieu of cash overtime can be made a condition of initial employment as long as use of comp time is clearly communicated to the employee and the comp time policy is consistent with the Act. 29 C.F.R. § 553.23(c). For other employees, receipt of a written notice regarding the use of comp time and the absence of any objection from the employee are sufficient to establish the necessary agreement or understanding.

An employer need not make compensatory time off available to all employees and need not have the same comp time agreement with all employees. 29 C.F.R. § 553.23(c). The use of comp time in lieu of cash overtime can be restricted to certain hours of work. 29 C.F.R. § 553.23(a)(2). Any combination of comp time and cash overtime payments can be used so long as the principle of time-and-one-half pay for overtime hours of work is maintained.

The compensatory time off that is earned by a public employee constitutes a legal liability for the employing jurisdiction. Employees generally may accrue up to 240 hours of comp time. Because comp time is accumulated at a time-and-one-half rate, the 240-hour limit represents only 160 hours of overtime work. Employees who work in a public safety activity, emergency response activity, or seasonal activity may accumulate up to 480 hours of comp time. As long as some of the employee's work regularly includes activities subject to the 480-hour cap, the employee is covered by the higher cap. Employers are expected in good faith to resist the temptation to assign clerical employees to periodic snow shoveling or ambulance work in order to allow them to accumulate more comp time.

The DOL has emphasized that comp time is not to be used as a means of avoiding the payment of statutory overtime compensation. A public employee has a right to use any accrued compensatory time off within a reasonable time after making a request for its use, as long as its use will not unduly disrupt the operations of the employer. An employee must not be coerced to accept more comp time than an employer can realistically, and in good faith, expect to be able to grant. 29 C.F.R. § 553.25(b). A public employer can require employees to use accrued comp time within reasonable scheduling limitations.

The employer may freely substitute cash, in whole or in part, for comp time as long as the substitution of cash is permitted by the comp time agreement. Such a substitution will not affect subsequent granting of compensatory time off in future workweeks or work periods. 29 C.F.R. § 553.26.

When employment is terminated, a public employee must be paid for unused comp time computed at the higher of the following:

- One and one half times the average regular rate received by such employee during the last 3 years of employment, or
- One and one half times the final regular rate received by such employee.

The phrase "last 3 years of employment" means the 3-year period immediately before termination, so that if an employee has a break in service, the period of employment after the break will be treated as a new employment. 29 C.F.R. § 553.27(c).

Compensatory Time Off for Private Employees

The use of compensatory time off for private employees is rendered impractical by the requirement that all comp time be used in the same pay period in which it is accrued. This requirement essentially limits the use of comp time to employers that use biweekly, semi-monthly, or longer pay periods. If an employee works overtime in a workweek that falls at the beginning of a pay period, then the employee can take time off with pay in a workweek that ends later in the same pay period. If an employee cannot use all of the accrued comp time by the end of the pay period, then the employee must be paid for the comp time in the paycheck for that pay period. Any comp time that is used by nonexempt employees must be provided at the rate of one and one half hours off with pay for every overtime hour that is worked. *There is no cost savings in the use of comp time.* An employer must be particularly careful to keep an accurate record of the hours actually worked by an employee and the hours for which an employee was paid when using comp time in lieu of overtime.

Compensatory Time Off for Exempt Employees

If an employer promises comp time to an overtime-exempt employee, the employee may be able to enforce the promise of additional compensation even though the employee was not entitled to overtime pay. Responding to an exempt employee's claim that he or she is entitled to comp time is often difficult because records generally are not kept of an exempt employee's hours of work. Providing comp time for hours in addition to an exempt employee's regular hours of work will not adversely affect the *salary* that must be paid in order for white-collar employees to be overtime exempt.

What Is an Employee's Regular Rate?

All overtime is computed as an additional one half of an employee's *regular rate of pay.* The regular rate is defined so as to ensure that overtime premiums reflect the true level of an employee's compensation. Basically, the regular rate includes *all* of an employee's compensation with certain narrow, statutorily prescribed exceptions. 29 U.S.C. § 207(e). Because the regular rate includes amounts in addition to an employee's base hourly wage, an employee's regular rate will usually be higher than the employee's base wage. The overtime pay of an employee who is paid a base wage of $10 per hour is best understood as $10 per hour for all of his or her hours of work and an additional half-time premium of $5 or more per hour for the hours over 40 in a week. Thinking of the overtime pay as a separate half-time premium makes it easier to understand how that premium is increased by bonuses, shift differentials, and the like.

For purposes of computing overtime, an employee's regular rate is calculated on an hourly basis, which will require converting monthly salaries, commissions, and noncash benefits into an hourly figure. The regular rate is calculated before any deductions are taken from an employee's wages. Thus, deductions for income taxes, payroll taxes, charitable contributions, and the misperformance of work will not affect an employee's regular rate.

The regular rate is calculated by separating all the compensation that an employee receives into three categories:

- An employee's regular compensation,
- Amounts that may be excluded from an employee's regular compensation but that *are not creditable* toward the overtime that is due, and
- Amounts that are excluded from regular compensation and that *are creditable* toward the overtime that is due.

Each of these categories is described below.

An employee's regular rate includes all hourly wages, salary, piece-rate compensation, commissions, shift differential, and standby compensation; the value of employer-provided meals and lodging; and all bonuses that are based on the quantity or quality of an employee's work. The regular rate also includes all of an employee's compensation that does not fall into the following two categories.

An employee's regular rate excludes amounts paid to pension and health and welfare plans; amounts paid on account of holiday, illness, vacation, or the failure to provide sufficient work; and amounts paid as reimbursement for expenses or as gifts. 29 U.S.C. § 207(e). Discretionary bonuses where neither the fact that any payment will be made nor the amount that will be paid is known in advance are excluded from the regular rate if the bonuses are not paid on a regular basis. The regular rate excludes prizes, such as for the referral of potential employees, where the employee who made the referral is not engaged in recruiting, the employee spent no time in learning the identity of the referral, the employee was not specifically urged to find referrals, and the employee learned the identity of the referral outside of regular work hours. 29 C.F.R. §§ 778.332, 778.333. The regular rate also excludes payments pursuant to certain defined thrift, profit-sharing, and stock option plans. 29 U.S.C. §§ 207(e)(3), 207(e)(8); 29 C.F.R. pts. 547, 549. As discussed in chapter 6, certain amounts paid to court reporters are also excluded from the regular rate of pay. However, none of these amounts that are *excluded* from the regular rate of pay can be credited toward the overtime that is due an employee. 29 U.S.C. § 207(h)(1).

An employee's regular rate also excludes overtime-like premiums. Amounts paid as premiums for hours of work that are in excess of 8 in a day, 40 in a week, or the regularly scheduled number of hours in a day's work are excluded from the regular rate. Premiums for work that occurs on weekends or holidays, or on a 6th or 7th day of work in a week, and premiums for work that occurs before or after a contractually established regular workday or workweek are also *excluded* from the regular rate. These amounts, however, *are creditable* toward the overtime that is due an employee. 29 U.S.C. § 207(h)(2). The premium pay for work that occurs on weekends, holidays, the 6th and 7th days of work, and before and after the regular workday and workweek *must be* equal to at least one half of the straight-time rate in order to be excluded from the regular rate calculation.

An employee's overtime rate must be calculated separately for *each* week of work. When an employee receives a commission, a bonus, or other compensation for work that was performed in more than one workweek, the compensation must be apportioned among the various workweeks for the regular rate to be correctly calculated. 29 C.F.R. § 778.209. An annual bonus that is paid at the end of a year would have to be apportioned over all of the workweeks in the year, and additional overtime pay would have to be calculated for those weeks during which the employee worked more than 40 hours, in order to meet the employer's overtime obligation.

The following three steps are used to calculate an employee's overtime for a particular week:

- The regular rate is calculated by totaling all of the compensation that must be included in the regular rate for the week and then dividing the total by the hours worked in the week.
- One half of the regular rate for the week is multiplied by the overtime hours in the week to calculate the overtime that is due.
- The employer can deduct any credits against the overtime that is due and then pay the balance.

By way of example, assume that in a week an employee is paid $10.00 per hour for 50 hours of work, receives $2.00 as a shift differential for 12 hours of work, and is paid $25.00 for being on standby. The employee's regular rate is the total of all of the employee's compensation, which is $549.00, divided by the 50 hours of work, which results in a regular rate of $10.98. One half of the regular rate, or $5.49, will have to be paid for each overtime hour of work. The total overtime due the employee for 10 hours of overtime will be $54.90.

If the employee had received an overtime-like premium for his or her work during the week in question, then the employer could have taken a credit for the premium and paid the balance that was due. For example, if the employee had received a premium of $5.00 per hour for 8 hours of work on a holiday that fell during the week at issue, then the $40.00 of holiday premium pay could have been deducted from the overtime due of $54.90, and the employer would have had to pay only the balance of $14.90. An employer may forgo a credit for any special overtime-like premiums that it pays if the employer does not wish to take such a credit.

As an exception to the manner in which overtime is generally calculated, an employer may pay employees on the basis of the wage rate that was in effect during overtime hours of work. 29 U.S.C. § 207(g). The *rate in effect method* can be used in two circumstances. Where employees are paid on a piece-rate basis, an employer may pay the employee one and one half times the piece rate that applies to the work performed during overtime hours of work. Where employees perform identifiably different kinds of work for which different hourly rates of pay apply, an employer may pay the employee one and one half times the hourly rate that applies to the work performed during overtime hours of work. To use such a pay plan, an employer must have an agreement or understanding with the employee regarding the terms of the pay plan before the performance of the work. If an employee is paid any amounts that must be included in the employee's regular rate of pay in addition to a piece-rate or hourly wage, then such amounts must be included when calculating the employee's overtime premiums.

If an employee is paid a fixed salary for all of his or her hours of work in a week, whether many or few, the employee's regular rate is determined by dividing the salary and any other additions to the regular rate by the total hours worked in the week. 29 C.F.R. § 778.114. One half of the resulting regular rate must be paid for the overtime hours in the week. If the employee's hours of work fluctuate from week to week, the regular rate will also fluctuate. To use such a pay plan, an employer must have an agreement or understanding with the employee that the salary will provide compensation for all hours of work, whether many or few. Accrued paid time-off benefits can be reduced for absences during the week, but reductions in salary generally cannot be made for partial weeks of work after paid time-off benefits have been exhausted. It may be possible to make occasional deductions as a disciplinary measure for willful absences or tardiness, but excessive deductions will invalidate the pay plan.

An employer can pay an employee a fixed sum as an employee's total compensation for varying overtime hours of work *only* if the employer meets all of the following requirements for use of a Belo pay plan:

- The amount of work that is available for an employee *cannot* be controlled by the employer or the employee.
- The total hours that an employee works from week to week vary above and below 40.
- An explicit agreement between the employer and the employee guarantees the employee a fixed number of hours of work each week or pay in lieu of work.
- The guaranteed hours do not exceed 60 per week.
- The agreement specifies the employee's hourly rate.
- The agreement provides a guaranteed number of hours of work that bears a reasonable relationship to the range of hours the employee actually works.
- The guaranteed amount includes the appropriate overtime premiums based on that hourly rate and the number of guaranteed hours.
- The employee is paid additional compensation at overtime rates when the employee works more hours than were guaranteed.
- The guaranteed amount is paid for every week in which the employee performs any work for the company.
- No deduction is made from the guaranteed amount for absences caused by vacation or illness, although accrued paid time-off benefits can be reduced for such absences.

29 U.S.C. § 207(f); 29 C.F.R. § 778.402.

State Overtime Obligations

States may impose more stringent overtime obligations than those required by the FLSA. For example, Alaska, California, and Nevada generally require that employees be paid time-and-one-half compensation for all hours of work in excess of 8 in one day. Wyoming requires daily overtime for women in certain occupations, and Oklahoma requires daily double time for women in certain occupations, but such requirements are of questionable validity. Florida requires additional compensation (not overtime) after 10 hours in a day for manual laborers, and Oregon requires that certain factory, mill, and cannery employees be paid overtime after 10 hours in a day. Colorado requires regulated employers to pay overtime after 12 hours in a day, and California requires essentially all employees to be paid double time after 12 hours of work in a day.

Under state law, the regular rate is *sometimes* calculated in a different and more expensive fashion than under federal law. In Alaska and California, a nonexempt salaried employee's regular rate is calculated by dividing the total regular compensation by the maximum number of straight-time hours of work in a week, which is usually 40. A nonexempt salaried employee must be paid *one and one half times* the regular rate for all overtime hours of work in such states. Some states may not permit the use of Belo pay plans.

Chapter 6

Is the Employee Exempt From the Receipt of the Minimum Wage or Overtime?

Limited exceptions from the FLSA's minimum wage and overtime obligations exist for white-collar employees and for employees in particular industries and occupations. Exemptions to the FLSA's requirements are construed *narrowly*, and the determination of whether an exemption exists is largely a question of fact. All employees are presumed to be entitled to overtime. The *burden of proving* that an employee is exempt lies with the employer. Exemptions contained in state wage and hour laws most likely will be construed in a similar fashion.

All overtime exemptions have four basic characteristics that must be kept in mind when evaluating the applicability of a particular exemption. The first characteristic is whether the exemption is limited to a particular *type of employer*, such as the limitation of the exemption for commission-paid employees to individuals who are employed by traditional retail and service establishments. The second characteristic is what *quality of work* an employee must perform in order to be exempt. In this regard, the executive exemption is limited to individuals who perform certain managerial tasks. The third characteristic is whether a particular *quantity of work* must be performed. For example, most of the agricultural exemptions require that an employee spend 100% of his or her time in agricultural work in a workweek. The fourth characteristic is whether any particular *form or amount of compensation* must be paid, such as the salary requirement for the white-collar exemptions.

In structuring its pay policies, an employer should bear in mind that overtime-exempt status is determined on an individual basis. The fact that some of the individuals in a job classification are overtime exempt will not be determinative of the status of all of the individuals in a job classification. If an employer classifies individuals as overtime exempt on the basis of their job classification, the employer must make sure that the job description is sufficiently narrow to ensure that all of the employees will be overtime exempt.

Following are the most common exemptions for executive, administrative, professional, and outside sales employees; the exemptions from both the minimum wage and overtime; and the exemptions only from the requirement to pay overtime. Set out last are the partial overtime exemptions, where overtime is required after a threshold other than the standard 40 hours per week.

White-Collar Exemptions

The most common exemptions are for *white-collar employees*, who are executive, administrative, and professional employees and outside salespersons as defined by the Secretary of Labor. 29 U.S.C. § 213(a)(1). An employee will be considered exempt if the employee performs *work of an exempt nature*, exempt work constitutes an employee's *primary duty*, and the employee receives *compensation* on a salary or a fee basis of not less than $250 per week (except for outside salespersons, for whom there is no minimum compensation requirement). Although

42

exemptions exist for executive, administrative, and professional employees who earn less than $250 per week, the terms of the exemptions are so restrictive that they are rarely, if ever, met. The requirements of the exemptions for employees who earn $250 per week or more are discussed below and are followed by an explanation of the compensation requirement.

Exempt Executive Employees

An individual will be considered to be an exempt executive under federal law if all of the following requirements are met:

- The individual's primary duty consists of the management of the entire business in which the employee is employed or a customarily recognized department or subdivision thereof,
- The individual's duties require the customary and regular direction of the work of two or more other employees, and
- The individual receives a salary of not less than $250 per week.

29 C.F.R. § 541.1.

An employee must be in charge of a department or other customarily recognized subdivision of the business in order to be an overtime-exempt executive employee. If an individual is not in charge of a department or subdivision, then the individual must meet the requirements of one of the other exemptions that are discussed below.

Management of a department is considered to include selecting, evaluating, training, and supervising employees. Setting employees' rates of pay and handling their grievances and discipline are also exempt managerial work.

Managerial work must constitute an individual's primary duty before the employee can be considered to be overtime exempt. An individual's *primary duty* generally includes those activities in which an individual spends more than one half of his or her time. 29 C.F.R. § 541.103. As a result, an employer must consider the actual amount of time that an individual spends doing exempt-type work when determining whether that person is overtime exempt. It is important to realize that the time an employee spends actively supervising other employees will be counted as time spent in exempt work; time spent merely being "in charge of the department" will be given less weight when evaluating an employee's exempt status. The determination of an individual's primary duty also includes a consideration of the relative frequency with which an individual exercises discretionary decision-making authority, the individual's relative freedom from supervision, the individual's relative rate of pay when compared with subordinates, and the like. An employer should be very cautious when classifying any white-collar individual as overtime exempt if the individual spends less than one half of his or her time actually engaged in exempt work.

Exempt Administrative Employees

An individual will be considered to be a minimum wage and overtime exempt administrative employee under federal law if the following criteria are met:

- The individual's primary duty consists of either of these:
  — Office or nonmanual work directly related to management policies or general business operations of the employer or the employer's customers, or
  — Academic administration that is directly related to instruction in an educational establishment;
- The individual's work regularly requires the exercise of independent judgment and discretion; and
- The individual receives a salary or compensation on a fee basis of not less than $250 per week.

29 C.F.R. § 541.2.

To qualify as exempt administrative work, the work must be of substantial importance to the operation of the employer. 29 C.F.R.

§ 541.205(a). The Department of Labor's regulations concede that there is no specific rule that delineates when work becomes of substantial importance to the operation of the employer. Although an individual need not be engaged in a policy-making capacity in order to be considered an exempt administrative employee, individuals who are not engaged in policy-making positions must generally carry out major assignments in conducting the operations of the employer and must perform tasks that affect the operations of the employer to a substantial degree. The Department of Labor's regulations make clear that clerks, bookkeepers, and other ministerial employees do not perform exempt work even though an error in their work may have substantial ramifications for an employer.

Recent court decisions have emphasized that an exempt administrative employee's duties must affect an employer's operations in a broad sense and that exempt employees cannot be engaged in production work. For example, television station producers, directors, and assignment editors; insurance appraisers and adjusters; probation officers and police investigators; escrow officers; and inside sales representatives have all been found to be production employees who are entitled to overtime. Conversely, marketing representatives of insurance companies, sales analysts for equipment makers, and customer service representatives of equipment manufacturers were found not to be engaged in production work. These employees were not engaged in production work because they did not underwrite insurance, they advised management regarding sales terms but did not sell equipment, or they were servicing customers who had previously purchased equipment, respectively. The breadth of the production exception and the fine distinctions made when the production exception is found inapplicable require caution when assessing the exempt status of administrative employees.

The Department of Labor's regulations also make explicit the requirement that an exempt administrative employee perform work that requires discretion and independent judgment. Those terms imply "that the person has the authority or power to make an independent choice, free from immediate direction or supervision and with respect to matters of significance." 29 C.F.R. § 541.207. Independent judgment and discretion should not be confused with technical skill in applying techniques or procedures; an employee who merely applies knowledge in following prescribed procedures or who determines whether specified standards are met is not exercising discretion and independent judgment. Employees whose work is performed in accordance with a detailed policy manual or operations manual are less likely to be overtime exempt. However, decisions that are made as a result of an individual's exercise of discretion and independent judgment need not be final decisions; they may be recommendations for action that are subject to review by another individual. Of course, if the recommendations are subject to extensive review and are regularly reversed, the individual who made the recommendations will not appear to function in an exempt capacity.

Exempt Professional Employees

An individual will be considered to be a minimum wage and overtime exempt professional employee under federal law if the following requirements are met:

- The individual's primary duty consists of the following:
  — Work requiring knowledge of an advanced type, in a field of science or learning, customarily acquired by a prolonged course of specialized intellectual instruction and study;
  — Work that is original and creative in nature in a recognized field of artistic endeavor, the results of which are primarily dependent on the employee's invention, imagination, or talent; or
  — Teaching in an educational establishment; and
- The individual's work requires the *consistent* exercise of independent judgment and discretion; and
- The individual receives compensation on a salary or a fee basis of not less than $250 per week.

25 C.F.R. § 541.3.

The learned professions are generally distinguished by the need for a bachelor's degree in order to perform the job. If more than one or two of the employees in a classification can perform the job without having obtained a job-related degree or can perform the work by virtue of on-the-job training, then it is unlikely that the employees will be exempt.

An overtime-exempt learned professional must be engaged in a recognized profession. Individuals who are engaged in general administrative or supervisory work or who are engaged in highly skilled manual work will not be recognized as professionals.

The dividing line between overtime-exempt artistic occupations and nonexempt technical and craft occupations is difficult to draw. For example, newspaper reporters who are given general assignments to complete are considered to be entitled to overtime even though they may have some choice in how a story is presented and how to get the information necessary to complete the story. But a newspaper columnist who has a wide choice of subject matter, style of expression, and opinion to be expressed is considered to be overtime exempt. Similarly, graphic artists who are given a particular subject to illustrate and some guidelines as to the format of the illustration are not considered to be overtime exempt. However, an artist who is given no more than the subject for a painting may be considered overtime exempt.

The overtime-exempt status of teachers in public schools is generally judged by whether or not they are certified to teach. 29 C.F.R. § 541.302(g)(3). A teacher's devotion of substantial time to extracurricular activities, such as coaching athletics, will not affect the teacher's exempt status.

An overtime-exempt professional must *consistently* exercise independent judgment and discretion. This requirement emphasizes that an overtime-exempt professional employee performs work of a varied, intellectual, or creative nature.

Highly Skilled
Computer Occupations

Employees who are engaged in highly skilled computer occupations are minimum wage and overtime exempt if they meet these criteria:

- Their primary duty consists of the following:
  - The application of systems analysis skills to determine hardware, software, or system function specifications;
  - The design, analysis, testing, or modification of computer systems or programs based on and related to systems design specifications;
  - The design, testing, or modification of computer programs related to machine operating systems; *or*
  - A combination of the foregoing that requires the same level of skill; and
- Their work requires the consistent exercise of independent judgment and discretion; and
- They are paid as follows:
  - On a salary or fee basis at a rate of $250 per week, *or*
  - On any other basis as long as their hourly rates of pay for a week are not less than six and one half times the minimum wage for all of the hours worked in the week.

29 U.S.C. § 541.303.

The exemption for highly skilled computer occupations was originally created by the DOL at the direction of Congress in 1990. The exemption is limited to work that requires highly specialized knowledge of the theoretical and practical application of computer operations. The exemption does not extend to individuals who have insufficient knowledge and experience to work independently in the tasks described or who are engaged in manufacture, repair, or maintenance work.

The compensation requirement can be met by paying a salary in the same manner and amount that applies to the other white-collar exemptions *or* by paying on an hourly or other basis as long as the employee's wages for a week are more than the required minimum amount for *all* of the hours of work in the week.

When the overtime exemption for computer professionals was reenacted in 1995, the hourly rate at which an employee had to be paid in order to be overtime exempt was fixed at $27.63 per hour. As reenacted, the exemption does not explicitly require the consistent exercise of independent judgment and discretion or explicitly require a particular level of knowledge in computer-related work, as specified in the DOL's definition of an exempt employee. The extent to which such requirements are an implicit aspect of exempt computer-related work remains to be clarified.

Some states limit use of the computer exemption. An employer cannot compensate overtime-exempt computer professionals on an hourly basis in those states that require overtime-exempt employees to be paid on a salary basis. In California, the minimum hourly rate of pay for an overtime-exempt computer professional was $42.64 in 2002, and the amount increases annually.

Exempt Outside Salespersons

An individual will be considered to be an overtime-exempt outside salesperson if all of the following apply:

- The individual is primarily employed for the purpose of making outside sales,
- The individual is customarily and regularly engaged away from his or her employer's place of business in making sales, and
- The total time spent at work that is *unrelated* to the salesperson's sales does not exceed 20% of the employer's customary workweek.

29 U.S.C. § 541.5.

Sales include both the sale of goods and the negotiation of contracts for the provision of services. An individual is engaged in sales only if the individual is directly responsible for consummating sales transactions. An individual who accompanies salespersons to demonstrate a product or service is not engaged in sales work. An individual who does promotional work to expedite another individual's sales is also not overtime exempt.

The *outside* sales activities that are considered to be of an overtime-exempt nature generally take place at a client's premises. An individual who is engaged in sales work at a fixed location, such as a residence or branch office, will not be considered to be engaged in exempt outside sales work.

There is a strict 20% limit on doing work that is totally unrelated to sales. This limitation on nonexempt work is not calculated as a percentage of the salesperson's time. Rather, it is calculated as a percentage of the typical workweek of employees who are entitled to overtime and who perform the same type of nonexempt work as does the salesperson. Thus, if the salesperson spends a portion of his or her time in routine clerical activities, then the limitation on nonexempt work will be calculated as 20% of the typical workweek of the employer's clerical employees.

Some work that is performed at an employer's premises or other fixed location need not be counted toward the 20% limit on nonexempt work. Thus, the time that an employee spends at an office in work that is "incidental to and in conjunction with an employee's outside solicitations" need not be counted against the 20% limit on nonexempt work. 29 U.S.C. § 541.503. Such incidental office work includes writing sales reports, revising an individual's catalogue, planning an itinerary, and attending sales meetings. Such office work can be counted as a sales-related activity only when the office work is directly related to that particular salesperson's own personal sales activities.

The Compensation Requirement

To be exempt from the FLSA's overtime requirements, an executive employee must be paid on a *salary* basis, and administrative or professional employees must be paid on a *salary* or *fee* basis. A *fee* is a fixed sum for a specific, nonrecurring project; hourly compensation is not a fee. 29 U.S.C. § 541.213. A *salary* is a fixed sum for all of an employee's hours in a week, whether many or few. 29 U.S.C. § 541.118. There is no salary or fee requirement for lawyers, doctors, medical interns, medical residents, or teachers. There are only limited circumstances in which an employer can reduce an employee's salary for those employees who must be paid a salary.

An employee's salary can be reduced on an *hour-by-hour* basis only for intermittent or reduced-schedule leaves that *must* be provided pursuant to the *federal* Family and Medical Leave Act. 29 U.S.C. § 2612(c). A salary can be reduced only for *complete* days of absence caused by vacation, personal business, illness, or incomplete initial or final weeks of employment. A salary can be reduced for complete days of absence caused by illness before sick leave benefits accrue or after such benefits are exhausted as long as some sick leave benefit is provided. A salary *cannot* be reduced for a *partial* week of work that is caused by a lack of work. A salary *cannot* be reduced for *partial* weeks of absence because of jury, witness, or military duty, but sums received for such service can be used to make up part of the employee's salary for the week.

An employer may, of course, use paid sick leave or vacation to make up part of an employee's customary weekly salary for a *complete* day of absence. Some courts and the DOL have declared that an employer can use paid sick leave and vacation benefits to make up for hours of work that were lost as a result of a *partial* day of absence, but there is no consensus on this issue. An employee's salary cannot be subject to reduction for absences on an hour-by-hour basis after paid-time-off benefits are exhausted, unless the absence is specifically protected by the Family and Medical Leave Act.

An employer may make deductions from an employee's weekly salary for the violation of major safety rules. However, partial-week suspensions or pay reductions for other reasons have been found to violate the salary pay requirement. Suspensions for an entire workweek do not violate the salary pay requirement.

The courts are divided as to whether providing extra pay for extra work constitutes a violation of the salary pay requirement. The DOL considers extra pay for extra work to be consistent with the salary pay requirement.

The salary pay requirement is violated when an employee is paid subject to the possibility of an impermissible deduction being made. A salary is paid *subject to* an impermissible deduction when there is a clear and particularized policy or actual practice of making impermissible deductions. Because the mere possibility that an inappropriate salary pay policy will result in an employee being paid less than what is required will destroy the exempt status of *all* of an employer's employees, it is particularly important that employers maintain a lawful salary pay policy.

It is very difficult to remedy any failure to meet the salary pay requirement by paying employees for improper deductions from their salaries after the deductions have been made. Most courts have permitted an employer to make retroactive payments to correct shortfalls in salary payments only where the employer maintained an appropriate salary pay policy and inadvertently failed to follow its own policy.

The extension of the salary pay requirement to public employers provoked a major crisis. Many public employers maintained *accountability* policies that resulted in deductions from pay for partial days of absence. As a result, many public employers failed to meet the salary pay requirement. After a tidal wave of litigation concerning public employees' salary pay status had engulfed the courts, the DOL provided some relief for public employers by revising the salary pay requirement. A public employer can reduce a salary for these reasons:

- Penalties imposed as a result of violation of a major safety rule;
- Complete days of absence for personal reasons and for illness before sick leave benefits accrue or after they are exhausted;
- Partial days of absence for personal reasons, illness, or injury when accrued leave is not used because of the following:
  — Permission to use the leave has not been received or has been denied,

— Accrued leave has been exhausted, or

— The employee chooses to use leave without pay; and

• Complete days of absence during initial and final weeks of work.

29 C.F.R. § 541.5d. Deductions from a public employee's salary for partial days of absence can be made only where the employee accrues personal leave and sick leave and where use of accrued leave for partial days of absence is pursuant to a law or practice based on principles of public accountability. Deductions still cannot be made for absences of part of a week caused by disciplinary suspensions; lack of work; or jury, witness, or military duty. Pay received from the government for jury, witness, or military duty can be offset against a salary. If a deduction in an employee's pay is made caused by a budget-required furlough, the employee's exempt status will be lost for the workweek in which the pay reduction is made.

Additional Exemptions From Both the Minimum Wage and Overtime Obligations

In addition to the *white-collar* exemptions, exemptions from *both* the FLSA's minimum wage *and* overtime requirements include the following:

Employees of Seasonal Amusement and Recreation Establishments

Employees of seasonal amusement and recreational establishments, organized camps, and religious or nonprofit educational conference centers are exempt from the minimum wage and overtime requirements of the Act. 29 U.S.C. § 213(a)(3). The establishment, camp, or conference center will be exempt if either of the following requirements is met:

• It does not operate more than 7 months in any calendar year; or

• During the preceding calendar year, its average receipts for any 6 months of the year were no more than one third of its receipts for the other 6 months of the year.

An establishment will qualify under the 7 months' test as long as it is not open to the public for more than 7 months out of a year. If an establishment is operated primarily with tax receipts by a public entity, the establishment cannot meet the average receipts test.

Employees Engaged in Fishing Activities

Employees who are engaged in the taking, propagating, harvesting, or farming of fish, shellfish, seaweed, or other aquatic life forms are exempt from the receipt of the minimum wage and overtime. 29 U.S.C. § 213(a)(5); 29 C.F.R. pt. 784. The exemption extends to the first processing of aquatic life at sea incident to the listed activities. To fall within the exemption, such processing must take place on the same ship that harvested the fish, shellfish, or the like. Traveling to and from the place of work and loading and unloading the vessel also are considered to be exempt work.

Small Agricultural Employers

An agricultural employee is minimum wage and overtime exempt where any of the following exists:

- The employer used fewer than 500 person-days of labor in every quarter of the preceding year, excluding work performed by members of the employer's immediate family.
- The employee is a member of the employer's immediate family.
- The employee is engaged as a hand harvester subject to particularized limitations.
- The employee is principally engaged in the range production of livestock.

29 U.S.C. § 213(a)(6). The exemption will be lost if the establishment in which the employee works is under common control with a supporting business and the gross sales of the combined businesses exceed $10 million per year. 29 U.S.C. § 213(g).

Employees Exempted by the Department of Labor

The Department of Labor may exempt limited classifications of employees in order to enhance their employability. Those classifications include the following:

- Full-time students in retail or service establishments, in agriculture, and in institutions of higher education;
- Student-learners in *bona fide* vocational training programs;
- Apprentices;
- Learners;
- Messengers; and
- Disabled workers.

29 U.S.C. § 214; 29 C.F.R. pts. 520, 525.

An application must be made to the DOL and a certificate received from it before the exemptions can be used. The employees will be overtime exempt only to the extent provided by the DOL. 29 U.S.C. § 213(a)(7). It is not unusual for states to grant exemptions from their minimum wage requirements that are *not* conditioned on obtaining a certificate from the state's labor law enforcement agency. However, if an employer is subject to regulation by the FLSA, such exemptions are of no value in the absence of a DOL certificate.

Employees of Small Newspapers

Neither the minimum wage nor overtime need be paid to individuals who are employed in connection with the publication of daily, weekly, or semiweekly newspapers of 4,000 or less in circulation. For the exemption to apply, the major part of the newspaper's circulation must be in the county where the newspaper is published or in the contiguous counties. 29 U.S.C. § 213(a)(8); 29 C.F.R. § 786.250.

Switchboard Operators

Switchboard operators who are employed by independently owned public telephone companies that have fewer than 750 stations are exempt from receipt of the minimum wage and overtime. 29 U.S.C. § 213(a)(10). The exemption will be lost in any week in which the employee spends more than 20% of his or her time in activities other than operating the switchboard. 29 C.F.R. § 786.100.

Seamen on Other
Than American Vessels

Seamen on other than American vessels need not be paid the minimum wage or overtime. 29 U.S.C. § 213(a)(12). For a description of what activities constitute the work of a seaman and how vessels are classified, please see the discussion below of the overtime exemption for seamen on American vessels.

Babysitters

Babysitters who are employed on a casual basis are exempt from receipt of the minimum wage and overtime. 29 U.S.C. § 213(a)(15); 29 C.F.R. pt. 552. A *babysitter* is an individual who provides custodial care and protection to minors in and about the home in which the babysitter is employed. A babysitter cannot spend more than 20% of his or her work time in any week doing housekeeping work that is unrelated to the babysitting. *Casual employment* means employment on an irregular and intermittent basis that does not generally exceed 20 hours per week. Any babysitter who is employed through an agency is not employed on a casual basis. Registered nurses, licensed vocational nurses, and licensed practical nurses as well as other trained personnel cannot qualify for the exemption.

Companionship Services

Employees who provide companionship services to individuals who are unable to care for themselves because of age or infirmity are exempt from receipt of the minimum wage and overtime. 29 U.S.C. § 213(a)(15); 29 C.F.R. pt. 552. Companionship services include the care and protection of an individual in the individual's home and housework that is directly related to the companionship services such as preparing meals, making beds, and washing clothes. The exemption will be lost if the employee spends more than 20% of his or her time in general housework that is unrelated to providing companionship services. The exemption may also apply to companions who work through agencies. Trained personnel, such as registered nurses, licensed vocational nurses, and licensed practical nurses, cannot qualify for the exemption.

Criminal Investigators

Criminal investigators who are employed by the federal government and who are paid availability pay pursuant to section 5545a of title 5 of the United States Code are exempt from the minimum wage and overtime that are required by the FLSA. 29 U.S.C. §§ 213(a)(16), 213(b)(30).

Homeworkers Making Wreaths

Employees who work at home and who are engaged in making wreaths that are principally composed of holly, pine, cedar, or other evergreens are exempt from the minimum wage and overtime requirements of the FLSA. 29 U.S.C. § 213(d); 29 C.F.R. pt. 780. The exemption includes harvesting of the evergreens or other forest products that the employees use to make wreaths. To be exempt in a week, all of the employee's wreath-making work must be performed in the employee's *bona fide* residence.

Newspaper Delivery Services

Employees who deliver newspapers directly to the ultimate consumer are minimum wage and overtime exempt. 29 U.S.C. § 213(d). The exemption may be lost if the employees deliver other materials, such as product samples.

Overtime Exemptions

The FLSA's *overtime* provisions *alone* do not apply with respect to the following employees:

Commission-Paid Retail and Service Employees

Employees of retail and service businesses who earn one and one half times the minimum wage and who receive more than one half of their compensation from commissions are exempt from the receipt of overtime. 29 U.S.C. § 207(i); 29 C.F.R. pt. 779. This exemption is limited to *traditional* retail and service businesses. A *traditional* retail and service business meets the everyday needs of the general public. Included in this concept are department stores, drugstores, and restaurants. Other employers, such as manufacturers, banks, doctors' offices, contractors, and the like, cannot use the exemption.

For the exemption to apply, the employee's compensation must exceed one and one half times the minimum wage for the hours that the employee has worked. As the number of hours that the employee works increases, so also will the minimum amount that the employee must be paid in order to be exempt.

At least one half of an employee's compensation over a representative period of time must consist of commissions. A *commission* is generally an amount that is calculated as a proportion of the cost of a good or service. The employer can select the representative period that is used to determine whether this requirement is met. The selected period must fairly reflect the earning pattern or regular variations in income of the employee. The period cannot be less than one month or longer than one year. The selected period must be identified in the employer's records.

Motor-Carrier Employees

The motor-carrier exemption applies to employees whom the United States Department of Transportation (DOT) has the power to regulate because such employees affect the safety of interstate transportation.

29 U.S.C. § 213(b)(1); 29 C.F.R. pt. 782. The exemption does not apply to classifications of employees over which the DOT has no jurisdiction or has specifically disclaimed jurisdiction, such as school bus drivers and ambulance drivers. The exemption does not apply to employees who are subject to regulation for reasons other than their involvement in interstate commerce, such as employees who are regulated by DOT because they are engaged in the transportation of hazardous materials.

Interstate transportation is the transportation of goods from one state *directly* to another state or the completion of an in-state link in a *continuous* chain of interstate transportation. If, when specific goods are shipped, the shipper intends the goods to be delivered to an identifiable out-of-state destination, the goods' transportation within a state as one link in a continuous chain of interstate transportation will be considered interstate commerce. However, the fact that some or all of the goods that are delivered to a warehouse will eventually be sold and shipped out of state does not make delivery to the warehouse a link in a chain of interstate transportation. The same principles apply to the delivery of goods to their ultimate destinations within a state after the goods have been received at a warehouse from out of state.

Only employees whose duties directly affect the safe transportation of goods can qualify for the exemption. Drivers and drivers' helpers meet this requirement. Mechanics who work on the safety-affecting aspects of vehicles, as well as loaders who have the responsibility for deciding how to load trucks in a safe manner, also qualify for the exemption.

To be exempt, an employee whose duties affect the safety of transportation must have a cognizable impact on interstate transportation. The impact of an employee's duties may vary with the nature of the employer's transportation activities. If the employer is a common carrier that makes transportation services available to the general public and the employer assigns interstate work among all of its drivers, then all of the drivers may be exempt, even though only 3% or 4% of the employer's work is of an interstate nature. If the employer is a contract carrier, which hauls goods only for specific customers, or is a private carrier, which hauls its own goods, then the employer's transportation activities may be more regularized, and a more direct relationship between an employee's work and the employer's interstate activities may be required. If, for any type of carrier, a driver is assigned to intrastate work to the exclusion of interstate work, the exemption will be lost. The DOL will generally consider a driver to be exempt for a 4-month period after a driver actually carries out an interstate trip or, in the case of a for-hire carrier, for 4 months after a driver becomes part of a pool of employees who may reasonably be assigned to an interstate trip. The DOL's position in this regard is based on the DOT's regulation of drivers' hours of service, and changes in the DOT's regulations may affect the DOL's enforcement policy.

Employers should be aware that drivers who qualify for the motor-carrier exemption may be subject to the DOT's medical examination, drug testing, and hours-of-service limitations. The employer's operations may also be subject to the DOT's safety requirements and to regulation by the Surface Transportation Board.

Rail-Carrier Employees

Employees of rail carriers who are subject to part A of subtitle IV of title 49 of the *United States Code* are overtime exempt. 29 U.S.C. § 213(b)(2). Up to 20% of an employee's time in a given week can be spent engaged in nonexempt work without jeopardizing the overtime exemption. 29 C.F.R. § 786.150. The hours of work of many rail-carrier employees are subject to regulation by laws that specifically regulate railroads.

Air-Carrier Employees

Employees of air carriers who are subject to title II of the Railway Labor Act are exempt from the receipt of overtime. 29 U.S.C. § 213(b)(3). Employees may spend up to 20% of their time in work that is not related to air transportation in a given week without losing the overtime exemption. 29 C.F.R. § 786.1. The hours of service of many air-carrier employees are separately regulated by federal law.

Outside Buyers

Outside buyers of poultry, eggs, cream, and milk need not receive overtime compensation. 29 U.S.C. § 213(b)(5).

Seamen

Seamen on American vessels are entitled to be paid the minimum wage for their hours of work but are overtime exempt. 29 U.S.C. §§ 206(a)(4), 213(b)(6); 29 C.F.R. pt. 783. A seaman's hours of work include all of his or her hours on duty, including the time spent working or standing by at the direction of a superior. An *American vessel* is a vessel that is documented or numbered under the laws of the United States. A *seaman* is an individual who, subject to the direction and control of the master of the vessel, is primarily engaged in aiding the operation of the vessel as a means of transportation. Officers, radio operators, engineers, cooks, and stewards may qualify for the overtime exemption. The exemption is lost if the employee spends more than 20% of a workweek in work that is unrelated to the transportation aspects of the vessel's navigation. Loading and unloading cargo and dredging work are *not* considered to be transportation related.

Announcers, News Editors, and Chief Engineers of Radio and Television Stations in Small Markets

The announcers, news editors, and chief engineer of a radio or television station are overtime exempt if the station is located in a small market. 29 U.S.C. § 213(b)(9); 29 C.F.R. pt. 793. An individual must be primarily engaged in one of the named occupations to be exempt. An *announcer* may introduce programs, read news, present commercials, and present similar routine material. A *news editor* gathers, edits, and rewrites the news and also may present the news. A *chief engineer* is the individual who primarily supervises the operation, maintenance, and repair of the station's equipment.

A *small market* is defined as one where the major studio of the employer is located in a city or town with a population of 100,000 or less according to the most recent decennial census. The exemption is lost if the city or town is part of a standard metropolitan statistical area of more than 100,000. The exemption is restored for cities and towns in standard metropolitan statistical areas of 100,000 or more if the city or town in which the broadcaster is located has fewer than 25,000 residents and is located 40 miles from the principal city in the metropolitan area.

Salespersons, Partspersons, and Mechanics of Vehicle Dealers

An overtime exemption exists for salespersons, partspersons, and mechanics of nonmanufacturing establishments that are primarily engaged in the sale or servicing of automobiles, trucks, or farm implements. 29 U.S.C. § 213(b)(10)(A); 29 C.F.R. § 779.372. To qualify for the exemption, an establishment must do no manufacturing, but need only be more than one half engaged in the sale or servicing of automobiles, trucks, or farm implements for their ultimate purchasers. *Salespersons* include those individuals who sell vehicles, but the definition does not include service writers. *Partspersons* include individuals who requisition, stock, and dispense parts. *Mechanics* include individuals who repair vehicles, but the definition excludes washing and nonmechanical preparatory activities. To be exempt, an employee must spend more than one half of his or her time in the designated activities.

Salespersons of Trailers, Boats, and Aircraft

Salespersons who are employed by nonmanufacturing establishments that are engaged in the sale of trailers, boats, and aircraft to their ultimate purchasers are overtime exempt. 29 U.S.C. § 213(b)(10)(B); 29 C.F.R. § 779.372. To qualify for the exemption, the establishment must be primarily engaged in selling the designated products. An employee must spend more than one half of his or her time in sales in order to be exempt.

Trip-Rate Drivers and Drivers' Helpers

Drivers and drivers' helpers who are paid on a *trip-rate* basis when making local deliveries and who do not work an average of more than 40 hours per week are overtime exempt. 29 U.S.C. § 213(b)(11); 29 C.F.R. pt. 551. A *trip-rate* basis of compensation is one that is based in substantial part on the number of trips, miles driven, stops made, or goods delivered. The exemption applies only after the DOL has approved the pay plan in question.

Employees Engaged in Agriculture

Employees who are engaged in agriculture are overtime exempt. Under the FLSA, agriculture has two components. 29 U.S.C. § 213(b)(12); 29 C.F.R. pt. 780. The first component, *primary agriculture*, consists of cultivating, growing, and harvesting crops as well as raising livestock, bees, fur-bearing animals, and poultry. The performance of primary agricultural work by a contractor on a farm, such as crop dusting, is also exempt work. The second component of agriculture, known as *secondary agriculture*, includes any practices performed by a farmer that are incidental to primary agriculture, such as preparation for market and delivery to storage or to market, or to carriers for transportation to market, even if performed off the farm. The performance of secondary agriculture by a contractor, such as threshing wheat, is exempt work only if it is performed on a farm.

The agriculture exemption operates on a week-by-week basis. If an employee performs any work that is not covered by the agriculture exemption or another exemption in a week, then the exemption will be lost for that week.

The limits of the agriculture exemption are difficult to define precisely given the many varied activities that take place in conjunction with farming. The exemption is most commonly lost in two ways. First, the exemption will be lost if an employee performs any work on products that have been grown off the farm in question. For example, where otherwise exempt agricultural employees spent only a few hours of their time preparing the products of other farmers to go to market, the exemption was lost. Second, the exemption can be lost if the agricultural products are processed beyond just being prepared for market. For example, if a farmer raises vegetables and then washes, cuts, and packages the vegetables for retail sale, the exemption will be lost for the employees who are engaged in the washing, cutting, and packaging.

Employees Engaged in Irrigation Activities

Employees who are engaged in the operation of ditches, canals, reservoirs, or waterways that are used exclusively for supplying and storing water, 90% of which was delivered for agricultural purposes in the preceding calendar year, will be exempt if the irrigation activities are operated on a nonprofit or sharecrop basis. 29 U.S.C. § 213(b)(12); 29 C.F.R. pt. 780. To be exempt, an employee must spend his or her entire week performing exempt irrigation work or another type of exempt work.

Employees of Agriculture and Livestock Auction Operations

In the determination of whether an employee spends his or her entire workweek engaged in agriculture, the time that an employee spends in related livestock auction operations will be considered to be exempt work. 29 U.S.C. § 213(b)(13); 29 C.F.R. pt. 780. An employee must be primarily or chiefly engaged in agriculture in a given week in order for the livestock auction work to be considered exempt work. The employee must also be primarily or chiefly employed in the week in question by the farmer who conducted the livestock auction operations. The livestock auction operations must be an ancillary portion of the farmer's agricultural activities. The employee must be paid at least the minimum wage for the time spent in auction work. If any of these requirements are not met in a given week, the employee will not be exempt.

Employees of Small
Country Elevators

Employees who are employed by small country elevators that market farm products, such as grain, for farmers will be overtime exempt if not more than five employees are engaged in the elevator's operations. 29 U.S.C. § 213(b)(14); 29 C.F.R. § 536.3. The exemption will apply even if the country elevator sells products and services that are used in operating farms. The exemption is limited to country elevators that receive 95% of their agricultural commodities from the immediate locale of the elevator. If an employee spends any portion of his or her work-week in nonexempt work, the employee will not be exempt in that week.

Employees Engaged in
Processing Maple Sap

Employees who are engaged in the processing of maple sap are overtime exempt. 29 U.S.C. § 213(b)(15); 29 C.F.R. pt. 780. The processing of maple sap includes the production of syrup and unrefined sugar.

Employees in Fruit and Vegetable
Harvest Transportation

The preparation for transportation and transportation of fruits and veg-etables from the farm where they were grown to the place of first processing or marketing is exempt work if the place of first processing or marketing is in the same state as the farm. 29 U.S.C. § 213(b)(16)(A); 29 C.F.R. pt. 780. An employee who spends his or her entire workweek in exempt work will not be due overtime under the FLSA. Retail packing, process-ing, and canning are not exempt work. Any transportation beyond the first place of processing or marketing is also not an exempt activity.

Employees Transporting
Harvest Workers

The transportation between a farm and any point within the same state of individuals who are or will be employed in harvesting of fruits or vegetables is exempt work. 29 U.S.C. § 213(b)(16)(B); 29 C.F.R. pt. 780. The exemption is limited to the persons who actually perform the transportation work; individuals who perform mechanical or office work for the transportation company are not exempt.

Taxicab Drivers

Taxicab drivers are overtime exempt. 29 U.S.C. § 213(b)(17); 29 C.F.R. § 786.200. If a cab driver spends more than 20% of his or her workweek in activities that are unrelated to driving a cab, the exemption will be lost for that week.

Employees of Small Fire Protection and Law Enforcement Agencies

Fire protection employees of public agencies with fewer than five such employees are overtime exempt. 29 U.S.C. § 213(b)(20); 29 C.F.R. pt. 553. A parallel exemption exists for law enforcement personnel when a public agency engages fewer than five such employees. The exemption operates on a week-by-week basis and will be lost in any workweek in which there are five or more employees, regardless of whether the employees are full-time or part-time or on leave or not. In those weeks in which the exemption does not apply, the agency may use the reduced overtime standard that generally applies to fire protection and law enforcement personnel of public agencies.

Residential Domestic Employees

Domestic employees such as cooks, maids, butlers, and chauffeurs who reside in the private household in which they are employed are overtime exempt. 29 U.S.C. § 213(b)(21); 29 C.F.R. pt. 552. Cooks, maids, butlers, and chauffeurs who work in institutional settings to provide services to the residents of the institution are not exempt. The exemption does not include individuals who work in businesses that are operated from private homes, such as professional offices that are maintained in a residence.

Couples Employed by Nonprofit Educational Institutions

Married couples are overtime exempt if both spouses are employed by a nonprofit institution that maintains a school. 29 U.S.C. § 213(b)(24). The couple must be paid at least $10,000 per year and must be provided board and lodging free of charge. The couple must be employed to serve as the parents of children who are orphans, of children one of whose natural parents is deceased, or of children who reside at the institution and are enrolled in its school. The exemption applies only while the children are in residence at the institution.

Employees of Motion Picture Theaters

All employees of motion picture establishments are overtime exempt. 29 U.S.C. § 213(b)(27).

Employees of Small Forestry and Logging Operations

An employer's obligation to pay overtime does not apply to employees who are engaged in planting, tending, or felling trees, or in transporting logs or other forestry products to a mill processing plant, railroad, or other transportation terminal. 29 U.S.C. § 213(b)(28); 29 C.F.R. pt. 788. The exemption is limited to employers that have no more than eight employees engaged in such activities, although the employer may have additional employees engaged in other activities.

Employees in American Samoa

The DOL has broad authority to regulate the overtime pay of employees in American Samoa through wage orders and regulations. 29 U.S.C. § 213(e); 29 C.F.R. pt. 697.

Work Outside the United States and Its Territories

An employee who spends an entire workweek outside of the United States and its principal territories is exempt from the minimum wage and overtime requirements of the FLSA. 29 U.S.C. § 213(f).

Partial Overtime Exemptions

Partial overtime exemptions exist for the following employees:

Employees of Health Facilities– "8 + 80" Pay Plans

A hospital or residential facility for individuals who are sick, aged, or impaired can pay overtime for hours worked in excess of 80 in a 14-day period of time only *if* the facility also pays overtime for all hours of work in excess of 8 in one day. Those hours in excess of 8 in a day for which overtime was paid need not be counted toward the 80 hours of work in a biweekly period after which overtime must be paid. A specific agreement with the employee to use such a pay plan is a prerequisite to its application. 29 U.S.C. § 207(j).

Public Fire Protection and Law Enforcement Employees

The FLSA's overtime requirements are somewhat relaxed for fire protection and law enforcement personnel. 29 U.S.C. § 207(k). Fire protection employees include firefighters, paramedics, emergency medical technicians, rescue workers, ambulance personnel, and hazardous material workers who are trained and responsible for fire suppression and who are employed by public fire departments. 29 U.S.C. § 203(y). To qualify as a fire protection or law enforcement employee, the employee must spend at least 80% of his or her time in such duties. Sporadic or part-time work in another capacity may not eliminate the use of the relaxed overtime standard, but any work in another capacity should be carefully monitored.

To use the exemption, a public employer must advise employees that a particular work period has been adopted and will be used to calculate the employees' overtime. The work periods and thresholds after which overtime must be paid are as follows:

Fire Protection Employees		Law Enforcement Employees	
Work Period	Overtime Threshold	Work Period	Overtime Threshold
28 days	212 hours	28 days	171 hours
27 days	204 hours	27 days	165 hours
26 days	197 hours	26 days	159 hours
25 days	189 hours	25 days	153 hours
24 days	182 hours	24 days	147 hours
23 days	174 hours	23 days	141 hours
22 days	167 hours	22 days	134 hours
21 days	159 hours	21 days	128 hours
20 days	151 hours	20 days	122 hours
19 days	144 hours	19 days	116 hours
18 days	136 hours	18 days	110 hours
17 days	129 hours	17 days	104 hours
16 days	121 hours	16 days	98 hours
15 days	114 hours	15 days	92 hours
14 days	106 hours	14 days	86 hours
13 days	98 hours	13 days	79 hours
12 days	91 hours	12 days	73 hours
11 days	83 hours	11 days	67 hours
10 days	76 hours	10 days	61 hours
9 days	68 hours	9 days	55 hours
8 days	61 hours	8 days	49 hours
7 days	53 hours	7 days	43 hours

An employer that adopts the relaxed overtime standard for fire protection or law enforcement employees must abide by the following special rules when calculating the employees' hours of work:

- Sleep time can be excluded from hours of work only if an employee is on duty for *more* than 24 hours and there is an agreement to exclude sleep time from work time;
- Meal time can be excluded from the hours of work of law enforcement employees only if they are *completely* relieved of duty, and meal time of fire protection employees can be excluded only if they are on duty for 24 hours or more; and
- An employee's early departure from work because he or she has been relieved by another employee can reduce the employee's hours of work only if such early departures are completely voluntary and are commensurate with an employee's early arrivals at work.

29 C.F.R. §§ 553.222, 553.223, 553.225.

Charter Activities by Employees of Local Electric Railway, Trolley, and Bus Carriers

The time spent in charter activities by employees of street, suburban, or interurban electric railways or trolleys or bus carriers need not be counted toward the 40 hours of work after which overtime is paid. 29 U.S.C. § 207(n). For such charter activities to be excluded from an employee's hours of work, the exclusion must have been the subject of an agreement between the employee and employer before such work was performed, and the charter activities must not be a regular part of the employee's work.

Transcription by Court Reporters

Court reporters who are employed by public agencies are not considered to be working for the purposes of the FLSA's overtime requirement when the court reporters are engaged in preparing transcripts if the following applies:

- The reporters are paid on a per-page basis at the maximum rate set by law on July 1, 1995, or at a freely negotiated rate with the party requesting the transcript; and

- The transcription occurs outside the hours that the employee performs other work, including those hours for which the public agency requires the employee's attendance.

Where the above conditions are met, the amount paid per page is also excluded from the regular rate of pay on which overtime premiums are calculated. 29 U.S.C. § 207(o)(6).

Employees Subject to Certain Union Contracts

Employees who are engaged under either of the following specific types of collective bargaining agreements are exempt from the receipt of overtime except as provided in the union contract:

- Contracts providing that employees will not work more than 1,040 hours in 26 consecutive weeks; or
- Contracts providing the following:
  - Employees will not work more than 2,240 hours in 52 consecutive weeks;
  - Employees will be guaranteed not less than 1,840 hours of work in the 52-week period or guaranteed not less than 46 weeks of work at the normal number of hours of work per week, but not less than 30 hours per week, in the 52-week period;
  - Employees will be guaranteed not more than 2,080 hours of work in the 52-week period; and
  - Employees will be paid overtime for all hours of work that are in excess of the guarantee, that are in excess of 2,080 in the 52-week period, or both.

The exemption applies only to a union contract where the employees' representative has been certified under the National Labor Relations Act. 29 U.S.C. § 207(b)(1), (2).

Employees of Wholesale or
Bulk Petroleum Distributors

A partial overtime exemption exists for employees of independently owned local wholesale or bulk distributors of petroleum products. 29 U.S.C. § 207(b)(3); 29 C.F.R. pt. 794. For such employees to be exempt, all of the following requirements must be met:

- The employer must be an independently owned and controlled local enterprise that is engaged in the wholesale or bulk distribution of petroleum products;
- The annual sales of the enterprise must be less than $1 million, exclusive of excise taxes;
- More than 75% of the enterprise's dollar volume of sales must be in the state where the enterprise is located; and
- Not more than 25% of the annual dollar volume of sales must be to customers who are themselves engaged in the distribution of such products for resale.

The employees of such enterprises may be employed in excess of 40 hours per week if the following requirements are met:

- They are paid not less than one and one half times the minimum wage for their hours of work in excess of 40 in a week, and
- They receive overtime for any hours of work in excess of 12 in a day or 56 in a week.

Employees Receiving
Remedial Education

Employers may require employees who do not have a high school diploma or the equivalent of an eighth-grade education to spend up to 10 hours per week in remedial education programs without paying overtime for the time spent in schooling. 29 U.S.C. § 207(q). The education program cannot include job-specific training. The employees must be paid their regular rate of pay for the time spent in the schooling.

Tobacco Auction Employees

Employees who are engaged in providing services incidental to the auction sale, buying, handling, sorting, grading, packing, and stemming of certain types of tobacco are partially overtime exempt. 29 U.S.C. § 207(m); 29 C.F.R. pt. 780. The exact activities that give rise to the exemption vary with the type of tobacco. Employees who perform the specified work will be exempt for 14 weeks in a calendar year, provided that they are paid overtime for such weeks for all hours of work in excess of 10 in a workday and 48 hours in a workweek. An employer that uses the exemption is limited in the other exemptions that it may use, but the employer may still use the white-collar exemptions.

Employees Engaged in Cotton Ginning, Cottonseed Storing and Handling, and Processing Sugar Cane and Sugar Beets

Employees who are exclusively engaged in providing services necessary to any of the following activities are partially overtime exempt for 14 weeks in any calendar year:

- The ginning of cotton at establishments primarily engaged in ginning cotton;
- The receiving, handling, storing, and compressing of raw cotton at facilities that are primarily engaged in such work, unless the facility is operated in conjunction with a cotton mill;
- The receiving, handling, storing, and processing of cottonseed at facilities that are primarily engaged in such work; or
- The processing of sugar cane or sugar beets at facilities primarily engaged in such work.

29 U.S.C. § 213(h); 29 C.F.R. pt. 780. Such employees must be paid overtime as described above for tobacco auction employees. An employer that uses this overtime exemption may not use any other overtime exemption.

Employees Engaged in Cotton Ginning

Employees who are engaged in ginning cotton for market in any place in a county where cotton is grown in commercial quantities are partially overtime exempt for 14 weeks out of a period of 52 consecutive weeks. Such employees must be paid overtime as described above for tobacco auction employees. 29 U.S.C. § 213(i); 29 C.F.R. pt. 780.

Employees Engaged in Processing Sugar Beets, Sugar Beet Molasses, and Sugar Cane

Employees who are engaged in the processing of sugar beets, sugar beet molasses, or sugar cane into unrefined sugar or syrup are partially overtime exempt for 14 workweeks out of a period of 52 consecutive weeks. Sugar processing employees must be paid overtime in the same manner that was described above with respect to tobacco auction employees. 29 U.S.C. § 213(j); 29 C.F.R. pt. 780.

Employees of Amusement and Recreational Establishments in National Parks, Forests, and Wildlife Refuges

A partial overtime exemption applies to employees of private employers that operate amusement and recreation establishments under contract with the Secretary of the Interior or the Secretary of Agriculture in national parks, national forests, and land within the National Wildlife Refuge System. 29 U.S.C. § 213(b)(29). Such employees must be paid overtime after 56 hours of work in a week.

Public Employees on Special Detail

If a law enforcement or fire protection employee of an interstate, state, or local agency volunteers to be employed in similar activities on a special detail by a separate and independent employer, the time spent working on the special detail may be excluded from the number of hours after which overtime is normally due the employee. 29 U.S.C. § 207(p)(1); 29 C.F.R. pt. 553. The exclusion for work that is performed on a special detail applies even if the agency requires that its employees be hired by a separate and independent employer to perform the special detail work, facilitates such employment, or otherwise affects the conditions under which the special detail work is performed.

Public Employees Engaged in Occasional or Sporadic Employment

The time spent by employees of interstate, state, and local public agencies while voluntarily engaged in part-time or sporadic employment for their employers in capacities different from those in which the employees are regularly employed need not be counted toward the threshold after which overtime must be paid. 29 U.S.C. § 207(p)(2); 29 C.F.R. pt. 553.

Public Employees Substituting for Coworkers

If an employee of an interstate, state, or local public agency volunteers to work for a coworker who is engaged in the same type of work, during the coworker's scheduled work hours, the time spent substituting for the coworker need not be counted toward the number of hours after which overtime pay is due. 29 U.S.C. § 207(p)(3); 29 C.F.R. pt. 553. Any such substitution must be done with the approval of the employer.

Exemptions From State Obligations

Before ceasing to pay overtime to any employee, an employer must determine that the employee is exempt from both federal *and* state law. In some cases, the exemption from a state's overtime obligation may be different from the exemption that applies to an employee under federal law. For example, Nevada provides an overtime exemption for any employee who is paid more than one and one half times the state's minimum wage, and Hawaii provides an overtime exemption for any employee who is guaranteed compensation of $1,250 per month or more. In many cases, however, state law is more restrictive than federal law, and an employee who is exempt from federal law must still be paid the overtime premiums that are required by state law. For example, Washington and New Jersey have severely limited or eliminated the exemptions for drivers. Other states, such as Nebraska and Tennessee, have no overtime laws.

Chapter 7

WHEN IS CHILD LABOR PERMITTED?

The Fair Labor Standards Act prohibits the use of oppressive child labor and regulates the hours that children may permissibly work. 29 U.S.C. § 212. The monetary penalties for violating the child labor provisions of the act have steadily risen in amount. 29 C.F.R. pt. 579.

Employers should be particularly aware that the states frequently regulate the employment of minors. The occupations in which children are allowed to work and the hours they are permitted to work may vary significantly between state and federal law. States may require permits to employ minors even though the FLSA has no such requirement. Strict compliance with both federal and state law must always be observed with respect to the employment of minors.

The FLSA regulates the employment of individuals who are less than 18 years of age. 29 C.F.R. pt. 570. For regulatory purposes, children are generally divided into three groups by age: 16- and 17-

year-olds, 14- and 15-year-olds, and all younger children. The occupations in which children may work and the hours that they may work vary by group. Special rules exist for employment in agricultural occupations, and a limited number of occupations are exempt from regulation.

Employment of Minors Outside Agriculture

Work in any occupation except those viewed as particularly hazardous by the DOL is permitted for 16- and 17-year olds. *Particularly hazardous occupations* include those involved with the following:

- Establishments manufacturing or storing explosives or articles containing explosive components;
- Acting as a motor vehicle driver or outside helper, except for infrequent driving of brief scope during daylight hours by a 17-year-old employee who has a valid license, has passed a driver's education course, uses a seat belt, and drives a vehicle of less than 6,000 pounds gross weight;
- Mining of coal and other substances;
- Logging and working in saw, lathe, shingle, and cooperage stock mills;
- Operation of power-driven woodworking machines;
- Possibly being exposed to radioactive substances;
- Operation of power-driven hoisting apparatus;
- Operation of power-driven metal forming, punching, and shearing machines;
- Operation of power-driven meat processing machines, and occupations involved in the slaughtering, packing, processing, and rendering of meat;
- Operation of bakery machines;
- Operation of paper products machines, except for the operation of scrap paper balers and paper box compactors that are equipped with particular safety precautions;

- Operations involved in the manufacture of brick, tile, and similar products;
- Operation of circular and band saws and guillotine shears;
- Wrecking, demolition, and ship-breaking occupations;
- Roofing operations; and
- Excavation operations.

29 C.F.R. §§ 570.50, *et seq.* Some variation is permitted for minors who are enrolled in sanctioned apprenticeship programs and in school-sponsored student-learner programs. There are no limitations on the hours that 16- and 17-year-olds may work.

The employment of 14- and 15-year-olds is much more restricted than the employment of older children. Thus, 14- and 15-year-olds may not do the following types of work:

- Manufacturing, mining, or processing occupations or work in areas where manufacturing, mining, or processing take place;
- Working with any power-driven machinery or hoisting equipment except office machines;
- Operating motor vehicles or working as a helper on such vehicles;
- Working in public messenger service;
- Working in any of the occupations found hazardous for 16- and 17-year-olds; and
- Working in transportation, warehousing, communications, public utilities, and construction occupations except to perform office-clerical work in office settings.

29 C.F.R. § 570.33.

The following types of work are permitted for 14- and 15-year olds in retail, food service, and gasoline establishments:

- Performing office and clerical work;
- Cashiering, selling, window trimming, and comparative shopping;

- Price marking, assembling orders, shelving, bagging, and carrying out orders;
- Performing errand and delivery work;
- Performing cleanup work, provided that it does not include the use of power-driven mowers or cutters;
- Performing kitchen work, including the use of most home-type appliances but excluding the use or cleaning of the equipment listed below;
- Dispensing gas and oil and washing and polishing cars, but excluding any use of service pits, racks, or lifting apparatus; and
- Cleaning vegetables and fruits and wrapping, labeling, and stocking goods outside of freezers, meat coolers, and areas where meat is prepared.

29 C.F.R. § 570.34. The FLSA prohibits 14- and 15-year-olds from any work in retail, food service, or gasoline service establishments that involves the following:

- Working in or around boiler or engine rooms;
- Maintaining and repairing equipment and facilities;
- Outside window washing from window sills and using ladders or scaffolds;
- Cooking, except at soda fountains, lunch counters, snack bars, or cafeteria serving counters, and baking;
- Using or cleaning power-driven food slicers and grinders, food choppers and cutters, and baking machinery;
- Working in freezers and meat coolers and all areas where meat is prepared;
- Loading and unloading railroad cars, trucks, and conveyors; and
- All occupations in warehouses except office-clerical work.

Working as attendants at professional sports events is permitted for 14- and 15- year olds so long as they do not work:

- During school hours;
- Before 7 A.M. or after 7 P.M. from Labor Day through June 1, and after 9 P.M. from June 1 through Labor Day;
- More than 18 hours during school weeks;
- More than 3 hours on school days;
- More than 40 hours per week in nonschool weeks; and
- More than 8 hours on nonschool days.

29 C.F.R. § 570.35. Some variation from these occupational and hours-of-work limitations is provided for school-sponsored work experience and career exploration programs.

Employment of Minors in Agriculture

Children aged 16 years or older may work at any time in any farm job. Children younger than 16 years may be employed in agricultural occupations except those that the DOL has declared to be particularly hazardous. Hazardous occupations include those that use virtually any power-driven equipment and tools; work around bulls, boars, stud horses, sows with suckling pigs, and cows with newborn calves; felling or working with lumber of more than 6 inches in diameter; working from a ladder or scaffold more than 20 feet above the ground; driving passengers; riding as a helper or passenger on a tractor; working inside silos in many circumstances; and handling dangerous fungicides, rodenticides, anhydrous ammonia, and explosives. Some variations from these limitations exist for student learners in *bona fide* vocational agriculture programs and for minors who have completed 4-H federal extension service training programs or federally approved vocational agriculture training programs. All permitted agricultural employment must be outside school hours. 29 U.S.C. §213(c); 29 C.F.R. §§ 570.70 *et seq.*

With the written consent of a parent or guardian or on the same farm where a parent or guardian is employed, 12- and 13-year-olds may be employed in nonhazardous agricultural occupations. Any such work must be outside school hours.

Children younger than 12 years of age may work outside school hours in nonhazardous farm jobs with their parents' written consent but only on farms where employees do not have to be paid the minimum wage.

Only if the DOL has issued a waiver will 10- and 11-year-olds be permitted to work in nonhazardous occupations outside of school hours to hand harvest short-season crops. 29 C.F.R. pt. 575.

A child of any age may work at any time in any farm job on a farm that is owned and operated by the child's parents. 29 U.S.C. § 213(c)(2).

Child Labor Exemptions

The following occupations are exempt from the child labor regulations:

- Delivering newspapers to consumers;
- Acting in motion pictures and theater, radio, and television productions;
- Performing work for the child's parents, except in manufacturing, mining, or hazardous jobs outside agriculture;
- Making wreaths at home out of natural holly or evergreens and harvesting the materials that the child will use to make the wreaths; and
- Working outside the United States and its principal territories for entire workweeks.

29 U.S.C. §§ 203(l)(1), 213(c), 213(d), 213(f).

Recordkeeping

Employers of minors must keep a record of children's dates of birth in addition to the records that are customarily maintained for employees. Employers may avoid potential disputes regarding minors' ages by maintaining state employment or age certificates in the states where they are issued or by acquiring wage certificates from the DOL in those states that do not issue age or employment certificates.

State Regulation of Minors' Employment

Many states comprehensively regulate the jobs in which minors can be employed and the occupations in which they may work. Some states require a specific permit to employ a child. Obtaining a state permit to employ a child does not guarantee that the federal child labor laws will be met.

Chapter 8

WHAT IS THE EQUAL PAY OBLIGATION?

The FLSA requires that employees be paid equal wages, regardless of their sex, for jobs that require equal skill, effort, and responsibility and that are performed under similar working conditions. 29 U.S.C. § 206(d). The equal pay standard applies to all employees of an employer that has employees who are subject to the minimum wage provisions of the Act. The scope and limitations of the equal pay obligation are, in many regards, significantly different from an employer's other obligations under the FLSA.

The equal pay obligation extends to all compensation that is provided by an employer. In this regard, *compensation* includes hourly wage rates, commissions, salaries, and bonuses. Fringe benefits such as vacation pay and health benefits are also included in the equal pay obligation.

The equal pay obligation applies to all employees without regard to the minimum wage and overtime exemptions. As a result, executive, administrative, and professional employees must be paid equally, regardless of their sex, for equal work.

The obligation to provide equal pay applies to any jobs that are substantially equal; the jobs do not have to be exactly the same. The equal pay obligation is based on the requirements of the jobs and not on the skills that the employees possess.

The equal pay obligation applies only among employees who are employed at the same physical establishment. An employee cannot raise an equal pay claim on the basis of greater wages that are paid to a peer at a different physical location.

The obligation to provide equal pay does not apply where the difference in pay is caused by a seniority system, a merit system, or a system that measures pay by the quality or quantity of production. The equal pay obligation also does not apply where the pay differential is caused by any factor other than sex.

Employees who raise equal pay claims are entitled to the same protection against discrimination and retaliation as employees who raise other claims under the FLSA. In addition, an employer cannot reduce any employee's wage rate in order to attain compliance with the equal pay obligation.

The equal pay provision of the FLSA is administered by the United States Equal Employment Opportunity Commission. However, any remedy that is sought under the equal pay provisions of the FLSA must be pursued in the same manner as any other claim under the Act. An employee who prevails on an equal pay claim is entitled to liquidated damages and attorneys' fees in the same manner as an employee who prevails on a minimum wage or overtime claim. An employer may raise essentially the same defenses to an equal pay claim as can be raised with respect to a minimum wage or overtime claim, with the exception of the exemptions from the receipt of statutory wages.

Chapter 9

WHAT WAGE PAYMENT OBLIGATIONS EXIST?

All wages required by the FLSA are considered to be due on the pay-day for the pay period in which the wages were earned. 29 C.F.R. pt. 531. If wages are not paid on the designated payday, the employee may be entitled to liquidated damages. The FLSA does not specifically prescribe how frequently paydays must occur. With the exception of the credits that are permitted against the minimum wage, all wage payments must be made in cash or its equivalent.

The FLSA does not specifically prohibit deductions from employees' wages. However, deductions other than those required by law may not reduce an employee's wages below the minimum wage or reduce the overtime payments that are due on the basis of employee's prede-duction regular rate. Deductions from the salaries of overtime-exempt white-collar employees may affect their exempt status.

The FLSA leaves a number of wage payment obligations to regulation by state law. These areas include the frequency with which wages must be paid, the timing of final wage payments, and permissible deductions from wages. The states may regulate the provision of vacation pay, the maximum number of hours that employees may work, and rest periods and meal periods. The states may also set higher minimum wage and overtime requirements than are imposed by the FLSA. The states' ability to regulate such matters is limited only with respect to a few industries, such as railroads and offshore shipping, which are comprehensively regulated by the federal government.

Chapter 10

WHAT RECORDS MUST BE KEPT?

An employer has an independent obligation under the FLSA to maintain accurate records of employees' hours of work and compensation. 29 U.S.C. § 211. The obligation to maintain accurate records is the employer's. An employer cannot excuse its obligation to keep accurate records by delegating the responsibility to employees. An employer's failure to maintain accurate records will impose upon it an often insurmountable burden to disprove what an employee claims to have been his or her actual hours of work.

The Basic Recordkeeping Obligation

The records that must be kept vary somewhat with the nature of an employee's work. 29 C.F.R. pt. 516. The basic recordkeeping obligation of the employer for employees who are entitled to overtime includes the following:

- Name;
- Home address;
- Date of birth if under 19;
- Occupation in which employed;
- Sex;
- Time of day and day of week on which workweek begins;
- Hours worked each day and total hours worked each week;
- All inclusions and exclusions from the regular rate;
- Total straight-time and overtime earnings as well as deductions from earnings; and
- Date of payment, amount of payment, and period included in payment.

All basic earning records should be kept for 3 years. Time cards should be kept for 2 years.

An employer must keep those records that are necessary to substantiate specific overtime exemptions. For example, an employer must keep the commission pay plan and a record of the commissions paid to employees who are considered to be overtime-exempt commission-paid employees of retail and service establishments. For overtime-exempt executive, administrative, professional, and outside sales employees, an employer must keep the records set out above, with the exception of those recording hours of work, inclusions and exclusions from the regular rate, and overtime paid. 29 C.F.R. pt. 516.

States may impose more stringent recordkeeping and record retention requirements. In addition to the above information, California requires that an employee's time card show the exact time at which each period of work and meal period begins and ends, and requires time cards to be retained for 3 years.

Posting Requirements

Employers must post the DOL's notice regarding the FLSA's provisions.

Chapter 11

HOW ARE THE WAGE AND HOUR LAWS ENFORCED?

The Fair Labor Standards Act can be enforced by the Department of Labor or by an employee who has been adversely affected by an employer's pay practices.

Enforcement of the Wage Payment Obligations by the Secretary of Labor

Investigation by the Department of Labor

The FLSA is administratively enforced by the Wage and Hour Division of the United States Department of Labor. Field agents of the DOL respond to complaints by employees, unions, or competitors, or they simply conduct random audits of employers in a particular area. The

DOL has a recognized informant privilege that allows it to decline to disclose who has filed a complaint.

If a field agent discovers what the DOL contends is a violation of the Act, the agent will advise the employer of the DOL's concerns in an attempt to obtain voluntary compliance with the Act. The agent also will request back pay to be granted to the affected employees. If a settlement cannot be reached with the field agent, the Solicitor of Labor will commence an action for injunctive relief or for damages in federal court.

The FLSA authorizes the direct entry of agents of the federal government into places of employment to inspect records and question employees. 29 U.S.C. § 211. The United States Supreme Court has interpreted the Fourth Amendment's prohibition against unreasonable searches and seizures as limiting the right of federal agents to enter the workplace when the employer has an expectation of privacy. Such an expectation of privacy cannot be maintained in comprehensively regulated industries such as the production of firearms, the sale of alcoholic beverages, or mining. Furthermore, employers who have contracts with the federal government may have signed away the opportunity to assert their Fourth Amendment rights.

An employer that has not waived or lost its Fourth Amendment rights may insist that the DOL obtain a search warrant before entering the employer's premises in order to observe its operations. However, the DOL can require an employer to produce its records for inspection by issuing an administrative subpoena. 29 U.S.C. § 209. An employer may question the reasonableness of a subpoena through a court petition before suffering any penalty for failing to comply with it.

Interference with a duly conducted DOL investigation is prohibited. 29 U.S.C. § 211. Interference includes, but is not limited to, misrepresenting an employee's duties, hours of work, or compensation, or encouraging employees to make such misrepresentations. Submission of inaccurate time or wage records to the DOL may also be a criminal violation of the federal False Statement Act. 18 U.S.C. § 1001.

Injunction Actions

The DOL can bring an action on its own behalf to enjoin an employer's violation of the FLSA. Actions to restrain the violation of the Act may include compelling the payment of past due compensation to all employees, enjoining future violations of the Act, and prohibiting the sale or distribution of goods that were manufactured in violation of the Act. 29 U.S.C. § 217.

As the plaintiff, the DOL normally bears the burden of proving that additional wages or overtime payments are due. However, an employer bears the burden of pleading and proving that an employee is exempt from the receipt of overtime or any of the other defenses discussed below.

The burden of proof will shift to an employer if it has failed to keep the records required by the Act and an employee testifies to performing hours of work for which no compensation was provided. As a practical matter, it is often exceptionally difficult to prove that an employee is not exaggerating his or her wage claim when no records have been kept. Courts have repeatedly held that uncertainty as to the amount of an employee's unpaid wages does not preclude an award of damages. Increasingly, courts have been willing to hold that some employees have not been compensated for all of their hours of work even when the employees do not appear or testify at trial.

The significance of an injunction that requires an employer to obey the law in the future lies in the fact that any violation of the injunction may be enforced through a civil or criminal contempt proceeding. An employer that violates an injunction may be subject to fine or imprisonment in addition to payment of past due wages and possibly attorneys' fees.

Damage Actions

The Secretary of Labor has the option of suing for back pay and liquidated damages on behalf of specifically named employees. 29 U.S.C. § 216(c). An award of *liquidated damages* is an amount that is equal to any unpaid wages that are found to be due. Liquidated damages will automatically be awarded unless the employer can prove, as discussed below, that the employer had both a good faith and a reasonable belief that it was acting in compliance with the FLSA. The courts disagree as to whether interest can be awarded to an employee if liquidated damages are not awarded. An action by the Secretary of Labor for unpaid wages and liquidated damages will terminate an employee's right to bring the action. Some uncertainty exists about the effect of the filing of a suit by the Secretary of Labor on a previously initiated employee action.

Civil Money Penalties

The Fair Labor Standards Amendments Act of 1989 added a new penalty for employers that are found to have repeatedly or willfully failed to comply with the FLSA's minimum wage and overtime provisions. 29 U.S.C. § 216(e). A penalty of up to $1,000 for each violation may be assessed, and the assessment will be final unless appealed through a special administrative procedure. The penalty may also be collected through a court action or by deducting the penalty from amounts due the employer from the United States.

Civil money penalties may also be imposed for the violation of the child labor provisions of the Act. 29 U.S.C. § 216(p); 29 C.F.R. pt. 579. Penalties of up to $10,000 can be imposed for each violation of the child labor regulations. The penalties can be enforced in the same manner as the civil penalty for violating the minimum wage and overtime provisions of the Act.

Hot Goods Provisions

The FLSA includes two provisions that limit the ability to realize any profit or use out of goods that have been produced in violation of the Act. 29 U.S.C. §§ 212(a), 215(a)(1). The Act prohibits the shipment of any goods that were produced in an establishment in which violations of the child labor provisions occurred within 30 days prior to the removal of the goods from the establishment. A broader provision prohibits the offer for transportation, shipment, delivery, or sale of goods that were produced by employees who were not paid the minimum wage and overtime in accordance with the Act. The DOL has stepped up its use of the hot goods provisions in the garment manufacturing industry.

The acquisition of goods by payment of reasonable value for them in reliance on a written assurance that the goods were produced in accordance with the Act, and without actual knowledge of any violation of the Act, is not a violation of the hot goods provisions. The written assurance will not be sufficient if included in the contract or purchase order that preceded the production of the goods or if provided after the acquirer has otherwise obtained the goods.

Employee Enforcement of the FLSA

An employee may bring an action for violation of the FLSA in either federal or state court. 29 U.S.C. § 216(b). However, an employee of a state cannot sue his or her employer in federal court and can sue his or her employer in state court only if the state has waived its sovereign immunity. An employee who brings a wage action in federal court may join with it claims regarding the alleged breach of related state laws.

The ability of an employee to avoid an arbitration agreement and pursue a claim for overtime in court remains unresolved. No consensus exists as to whether employees are obligated to arbitrate FLSA claims under arbitration agreements entered into pursuant to the Federal Arbitration Act. 9 U.S.C. §§ 1, *et seq*. An adverse arbitration decision under a union contract may not bar a subsequent action for statutory overtime compensation.

An employee may, by specific statutory authority, bring an action on behalf of himself or herself and others who are similarly situated. 29 U.S.C. § 216(b). However, each employee must *opt in* to become a party-plaintiff by filing a written consent to sue with the court. The statute of limitations will continue to run against an employee until the employee files a consent with the court. The courts are broadening an employee's ability to notify other employees of such lawsuits and to solicit other employees to join the lawsuit.

As the plaintiff, the employee normally bears the burden of proving that there was improper compensation for work performed. An employer bears the burden of proving that an employee is exempt from the receipt of overtime. A plaintiff-employee bears the same burden of proof as the DOL and can obtain liquidated damages on the same terms that apply to DOL actions. In the absence of an award of liquidated damages, some courts will not order an award of prejudgment interest. A successful plaintiff is also entitled to attorneys' fees and costs in a reasonable amount.

Protection Against Discrimination and Discharge

Employees who have filed a complaint or instituted or caused to be instituted a proceeding under the FLSA or who have testified or are about to testify in such a proceeding are protected against adverse action for undertaking such conduct. 29 U.S.C. § 215(a)(3). These provisions have, on the whole, been construed quite narrowly, and generalized grumblings about wage payment practices will not be protected. An employee can pursue a retaliation claim against any person, including a manager or an employer that is so small as not to be otherwise subject to the FLSA.

Either the DOL or the affected employee may sue to enforce the right to be free of discrimination or retaliatory discharge. The remedies for impermissible retaliation include reinstatement, promotion, lost wages, liquidated damages, and legal and equitable relief. There is no consensus as to whether punitive damages can be recovered when an employee proves impermissible retaliation.

Defenses to Enforcement Actions

An employer may be able to assert as a defense that the employee was exempt from the minimum wage or overtime obligation. However, exemptions from the minimum wage and overtime obligations must be pleaded by the employer in its answer to the complaint and must be proven by the employer at trial.

An employer can avoid liability for minimum wages or overtime by showing that it acted in conformity with official written interpretations of the FLSA. The official interpretations of the FLSA are the regulations, interpretive bulletins, and advisory opinions that are issued by the administrative staff of the Wage and Hour Division of the DOL. 29 U.S.C. § 259. To prevail, an employer must show that it was aware of the DOL policy, it relied on the policy in good faith in structuring its payroll practices, its reliance on the DOL policy was reasonable, and it acted in conformity with the DOL policy.

An employer can avoid liquidated damages by pleading and proving that it had reasonable grounds to believe, in good faith, that it was not violating the Act. 29 U.S.C. § 260. For example, an employer may assert that it thought it was too small to be regulated by the Act or that it thought that the employee was performing more exempt duties. To show that it reasonably believed that its pay practices complied with the Act, an employer must show that it informed itself through appropriate references or knowledgeable consultants that the specific pay practices at issue conformed with the Act. Reliance on an attorney's opinion as to the conformity of a particular pay practice with the FLSA is a significant consideration in avoiding the imposition of liquidated damages. An employer that asserts it had a good faith and reasonable belief that it acted in compliance with the FLSA may waive the attorney-client privilege with respect to any previous advice regarding the issue. The court has the discretion to eliminate liquidated damages in their entirety or to partially excuse them.

The statute of limitations bars any claim for wages that were due on a payday that falls before the limitations period. The limitations period is measured backward from the date on which a complaint is filed in court. The statute of limitations for claims brought under the FLSA is 2 years, unless the employer's violation of the Act was willful, in which event the statute of limitations is 3 years. 29 U.S.C. § 255. A willful violation will be found where the employer either knew or showed a reckless disregard for whether its pay policy violated the FLSA.

Actions for equitable relief may be defended on general equitable principles. For example, an employee may be precluded from claiming compensation for unreported hours of work where the employer did not know and had no reason to know of the unreported work hours.

An employer cannot file a counterclaim against an employee in a lawsuit that is brought by the DOL.

A settlement of an FLSA claim without the approval of the DOL or a court is *not* binding on an employee. However, any amount that is paid to an employee for the specific purpose of resolving an FLSA claim can be credited against any amount that is later found to be due. 29 U.S.C. § 216(c).

Criminal Penalties

A violation of the FLSA that is *willful* in the sense that it is deliberate, voluntary, or intentional may be the subject of a criminal penalty. 29 U.S.C. § 216(a). The standard that is used to determine whether a violation is willful in a criminal sense is much more stringent than that which is used to determine whether a violation is willful for the purpose of extending the statute of limitations. Penalties for criminal violations of the Act include fines of up to $10,000. Imprisonment for up to 6 months can be ordered upon conviction for a second violation of the Act.

Enforcement of State Laws

Most states maintain specialized hearing procedures to resolve individual wage claims. Many states allow employees to pursue wage claims through class action in which all employees are included unless individual employees *opt out*. Such class actions are much more likely to include a large number of employees than the *opt in* procedure that is used under the FLSA. The state may also have longer statutes of limitation and civil and criminal penalty provisions that are more stringent than those provided by the FLSA.

Chapter 12

WHAT IS THE PREVAILING WAGE OBLIGATION?

A prevailing wage obligation is similar to the FLSA's minimum wage obligation, although the amount that must be paid as a prevailing wage is generally much higher than the minimum wage. The principal difference between the FLSA and prevailing wage laws is that prevailing wage legislation frequently requires the provision of locally prevailing fringe benefits or the payment of the cost of such benefits. A prevailing wage obligation is imposed on an employer when it has contracted to provide materials, services, or construction work under contract with the federal government or when it is a participant in certain federally funded programs. States frequently impose similar obligations on contractors that provide services or construction work for public entities.

Providing Materials or Supplies

The Walsh-Healey Government Contracts Act (WHA), 41 U.S.C. § 35, *et seq.*, requires that all employees engaged in providing manufactured materials or supplies to the federal government pursuant to contracts in excess of $10,000 be paid the locally prevailing minimum wage as determined by the Secretary of Labor. 41 U.S.C. § 35. The WHA does not require the payment of locally prevailing fringe benefits. The WHA requires that affected employees be paid overtime for all hours of work in excess of 40 in one week. The Act also imposes special child labor, convict labor, and safety requirements. The WHA does not apply to purchases that the government customarily makes on the open market, to perishable products, to purchases of agricultural products by the Department of Agriculture, to transportation pursuant to published tariffs, and to the provision of most telecommunications services. 41 U.S.C. § 43.

Providing Construction Work

The Davis-Bacon Act (DBA), 40 U.S.C. § 276(a), *et seq.*, requires that all laborers and mechanics engaged in the construction, alteration, or repair of a public work pursuant to a contract with the federal government in excess of $2,000 be paid an amount equal to the total of the locally prevailing wages and fringe benefits as determined by the Secretary of Labor. 40 U.S.C. § 276(a); 29 C.F.R. pt. 5. The obligation to pay prevailing wages and fringe benefits is generally limited to employees who work at the construction site, but it may, in limited circumstances, apply to batch plants, quarries, and other sources of supply. The DBA requires that all employees who are so engaged be paid at least weekly. The DBA applies to the principal contractor and all subcontractors who work under the principal contractor.

The DBA contains no overtime requirement. However, the Contract Work Hours and Safety Standards Act (CWHSSA), 40 U.S.C. § 327, *et seq.*, requires overtime compensation for all hours of work in excess of 40 in a week on all federally financed construction projects in excess of $100,000. 40 U.S.C. § 328. The CWHSSA also imposes special safety standards on covered contractors. Some contracts for transportation, telecommunications, and the purchase of supplies on the open market are exempt from the act. 40 U.S.C. § 329(b).

Providing Services

Under the Service Contract Labor Standards Act (SCA), 41 U.S.C. § 351, *et seq.*, all employees engaged in providing services to the federal government pursuant to contracts in excess of $2,500 must be paid the locally prevailing wages and must be separately paid the locally prevailing fringe benefits or an amount equal to those benefits. The amount and nature of locally prevailing wages and benefits are determined by the Secretary of Labor. 41 U.S.C. § 351; 29 C.F.R. pt. 4. Some contracts for the provision of transportation, telecommunication services, and public utility services are exempt from the act. 41 U.S.C. § 356. The SCA applies to, and imposes safety standards on, the principal contractor and all its subcontractors. The SCA contains a unique successorship provision that requires a contractor that replaces an earlier contractor to pay the wages and benefits required under the predecessor's collective bargaining agreement. 41 U.S.C. § 353.

Prevailing Wages Under Other Federal Acts

Prevailing wage obligations are imposed by various other federal laws, including such rarely encountered sources of regulation as the National Foundation on the Arts and Humanities Act. 20 U.S.C. § 951, *et seq.*

State Prevailing Wage Laws

Many states have statutes that require the payment of prevailing wages on state-funded construction projects. A few states have included the provision of some services under their prevailing wage acts. Although the preemptive effect of the federal wage acts has been debated, the consensus appears to be that states are free to regulate prevailing wages even where a federal prevailing wage standard applies. As a result, employers must comply with the more stringent of the two sources of regulation.

What Is the Prevailing Wage Obligation?

The obligation to pay the prevailing hourly wage applies only to hours worked in furtherance of a federal contract; the obligation does not generally apply to hours in a week or days spent in work unrelated to the federal contract. The hours spent on the federal contract should be separately identified on an employee's time card, and the amount paid for such work also should be separately identified. The amount paid in satisfaction of the prevailing hourly wage obligation should be stated separately from any amount paid in satisfaction of the prevailing fringe benefit obligation.

The prevailing wage rate for a particular task is not always easily identified. It is important for employers to consult with the DOL and the awarding body to determine the correct wage rate before a bid is made. An employer should not assume that the rate that most closely approximates its current wage rate is the correct prevailing rate.

A construction employee who handles the tools of a trade must generally be paid the journeyman's rate for the trade. The only common exception to the payment of the journeyman's rate is for apprentices who are engaged in the apprenticeship program for that craft. The long dispute over whether a reduced-wage helper classification would be recognized has resulted in rejection of such a classification.

The obligation to pay the locally prevailing fringe benefits requires providing the specified benefits, or benefits of equal value, or paying the equivalent cost of the benefits. Benefits that may be included in a prevailing wage determination include medical and life insurance, retirement benefits, disability and sick leave insurance, vacation and holiday pay, and apprentice training.

An employer can discharge its fringe benefit obligation by providing benefits of an equivalent cost to those that have been determined to be prevailing. However, the benefits that an employer provides must meet certain minimum standards before they can be credited against the fringe benefit obligation. Particular care must be taken with retirement plans (many profit-sharing programs may not qualify) and medical insurance plans (self-insurance poses special problems).

An employer can also discharge its fringe benefit obligation by paying its employees the difference in cost between any benefits that it provides and those that are required. The amount that is paid in lieu of providing benefits is excluded when calculating an employee's overtime rate. However, any amount that is paid in cash must be treated as wages for tax purposes. This factor will impose additional costs on the employer. In some cases, it will be necessary to provide the pay in lieu of benefits separately from the employee's wages.

An employer can challenge prevailing wage determinations made by the Secretary of Labor. Any such appeal must be made within a brief period after the wage rate is promulgated or the contract is put out to bid. An employer generally cannot dispute the wage rates in the course of a proceeding the purpose of which is to determine whether the employer has violated the prevailing wage obligation.

The DOL has taken the position that if any portion of an employee's work time is devoted to a regulated contract, then the overtime standard that the contract imposes applies to all of the hours that have been worked in the week.

Remedies for Failure to Pay the Prevailing Wage

The principal remedy for the failure to pay the prevailing wage is the government's withholding from the employer the amounts that are allegedly due the employees. The DOL may have to provide a hearing before a neutral fact-finder, either before any withholding takes place or shortly afterward. The exact means of contesting the withholding varies from statute to statute. Generally, a hearing is held before a DOL administrative law judge, after which an appeal can be taken to the Administrative Review Board or the Secretary of Labor and then to the federal courts.

Both employees and the DOL can bring an action for unpaid wages and benefits under the Davis-Bacon Act. However, only the Secretary of

Labor can bring an action to collect unpaid wages under the Service Contract Act and the Walsh-Healey Act.

The prevailing wage acts also give the government the right to terminate the contract of an employer that has failed to meet its obligations. Not only can the contract be terminated, but also the offending employer can generally be charged with the cost of finding a substitute contractor. See, e.g., 41 U.S.C. § 36. Violators of prevailing wage obligations can also be blacklisted for a period of 3 years. See, e.g., 41 U.S.C. § 37. Employers who appear on the blacklist cannot contract with the government for the prescribed time period.

Liquidated damages are payable under some but not all of the prevailing wage acts. The WHA imposes a $10 per employee per day penalty for violation of its child labor and convict labor provisions and allows the doubling of any wage underpayment as liquidated damages. 41 U.S.C. § 36. The CWHSSA provides a $10 per employee per day penalty for every day on which its overtime week obligations are not met. 40 U.S.C. § 328. An intentional violation of the CWHSSA is a misdemeanor punishable by a fine of up to $1,000 and imprisonment of up to 6 months. 40 U.S.C. § 332. In addition, management representatives who control the pay practices of an employer can be found personally liable for violations of the Walsh-Healey and Service Contract Acts.

Defenses to Enforcement Actions

The statute of limitations for prevailing wage claims varies with the act at issue and the forum in which the wage claim is litigated. Wage claims pursued in court under the Walsh-Healey and Davis-Bacon Acts have a statute of limitations identical with the 2- and 3-year limitations period that applies to the FLSA. 29 U.S.C. § 256. The DOL has successfully asserted that wage claims under the Davis-Bacon Act that are heard before administrative law judges have a 6-year statute of limitations. The Service Contract Labor Standards Act and the Contract Work Hours and Safety Standards Act also have a 6-year limitations period.

An employer may avoid liability for an alleged violation of the Walsh-Healey Act or the Davis-Bacon Act by proving that it relied reasonably and in good faith on an official written DOL interpretation of the obligations created by the act and that it acted in conformity with that interpretation. 29 U.S.C. § 259.